LAW EXPRESS: EU LAW

# EU LAW

2nd edition

Dr Ewan Kirk
Birmingham City University

**Longman**
**is an imprint of**

Harlow, England • London • New York • Boston • San Francisco • Toronto • Sydney • Singapore • Hong Kong
Tokyo • Seoul • Taipei • New Delhi • Cape Town • Madrid • Mexico City • Amsterdam • Munich • Paris • Milan

**Pearson Education Limited**
Edinburgh Gate
Harlow
Essex CM20 2JE
England

and Associated Companies throughout the world

*Visit us on the World Wide Web at:*
www.pearsoned.co.uk

First published 2009
**Second edition 2011**

ISBN: 978-1-4082-3800-4

**British Library Cataloguing-in-Publication Data**
A catalogue record for this book is available from the British Library

**Library of Congress Cataloging-in-Publication Data**
Kirk, Ewan.
  EU law / Ewan Kirk. -- 2nd ed.
      p. cm.
  Includes index
  ISBN 978–1–4082–3800–4 (pbk.)
  1.  Law--European Union countries.   I. Title.
  KJE947.K57 2011
  341.242'2--dc22

                                                          2010022302

10 9 8 7 6 5 4 3 2
14 13 12 11

Typeset in 10/12pt Helvetica LT Std Condensed by 3
Printed by Ashford Colour Press Ltd, Gosport

# Contents

# Supporting resources

Visit the *Law Express series* companion website at **www.pearsoned.co.uk/ lawexpress** to find valuable student learning material including:

- A study plan test to assess how well you know the subject before you begin your revision, now broken down into targeted study units
- Interactive quizzes with a variety of question types to test your knowledge of the main points from each chapter of the book
- Further examination questions and guidelines for answering them
- Interactive flashcards to help you revise the main terms and cases
- Printable versions of the topic maps and checklists
- 'You be the marker' allows you to see exam questions and answers from the perspective of the examiner and includes notes on how an answer might be marked
- Podcasts provide point-by-point instruction on how to answer a common exam question

**Also:** The companion website provides the following features:

- Search tool to help locate specific items of content
- E-mail results and profile tools to send results of quizzes to instructors
- Online help and support to assist with website usage and troubleshooting

For more information please contact your local Pearson Education sales representative or visit **www.pearsoned.co.uk/lawexpress**.

# Acknowledgements

I'd like to thank all those who helped by reviewing chapters, also Christine Statham at Pearson for her support, guidance and patience.

Finally, and most importantly, Penny.

## Publisher's acknowledgements

Our thanks go to all reviewers who contributed to the development of this text, including students who participated in research and focus groups which helped to shape the series format.

# Introduction

With the rapid development and expansion of the EU, it is becoming more important (if that is possible) for law students to get to grips with EU law. Rules and principles from the EU now affect an ever-expanding list of areas of law as powers are exercised and rules are made by the EU as a whole for the benefit of its Member States. It is also an area of law which is rapidly changing and has become very topical – the Lisbon Treaty is probably the most significant change to have occurred in the last few years, and has not been without controversy. Because of this, it is important to ensure that the sources you are using are as up-to-date as possible – older textbooks will have little or no reference to Lisbon and the changes this Treaty made.

The EU is also a very different system from the one you will have studied as part of your coursework on the English legal system. For this reason it appears daunting or 'scary' to many law students. However, this is not the case – EU law is, in some respects, more straightforward than the law in the UK, and a lot more linear. Students often make the mistake of attempting to draw parallels between the English Legal System and the EU system. Although there are some parallels that can be safely drawn, you should not fall into the trap of thinking that the EU is just like the system in the UK – they are very different. As the UK was not a member of the EU when it was originally formed, many of the legal principles will be different as they are based upon the legal systems of some of the original six Member States.

EU law, however, overlaps and connects with other subjects in such a way that it has an effect on just about every area of law you will encounter on a law degree, and therefore it is important to get to grips with the basics of the topic not only for the examinations you will have in this subject, but to help you to gain a better understanding in those other areas. As the areas in which EU law-making grows, so will the influence of this area in other subjects.

EU law can be broadly split into two general categories – first there are those aspects that concern the constitutional aspects of EU law, and secondly those that concern substantive elements of EU law (such as competition law, for example). You should bear in mind that no EU course will take you through all aspects of EU law, as there is such a wide range of topics covered, and much of the substantive law will appear in your other law subjects anyway.

This book aims to take you through the main areas studied by law students on LL.B degrees in the UK in the area of EU law, both concerning the way in which the EU legal system works, and substantive law subjects. EU law courses vary greatly between Institutions, however, so there may be some difference between the content of this book and the syllabus of your course. However, common areas of EU law are covered here, and so you should use this book for what it is – a guide to the main areas in this subject required for you to do well. A word of warning – it is no substitute for your textbooks, your lecture notes and other materials: instead this book should help you to focus in your use of those other materials.

Finally, as mentioned above, you should be very careful in your use of out-of-date textbooks in EU law – the law changed rapidly and significantly in 2009. That is not to say you shouldn't use wider materials – just be aware that if something was published prior to the accession of the Lisbon Treaty in 2009, it needs to be read in conjunction with a more recent book in order to ensure you are not using out-of-date law.

---

**REVISION NOTE**

Things to bear in mind when revising EU law:

- EU law is becoming more important as more powers are given to the EU and EU law affects other areas of law

- Don't think that the EU is just like the UK legal system – it is very different and has its own rules and traditions

- There are legal system and substantive aspects of EU law – make sure you check the syllabus of your course to see where you should focus your study of EU law

- Make sure that you make full use of your textbooks and lecture notes in order to understand the subject in depth – this book will not give you everything you need on its own

- Make sure you practise essay/problem questions, and get feedback on how you are doing

**Before you begin, you can use the study plan available on the companion website to assess how well you know the material in this book and identify the areas where you may want to focus your revision.**

# Guided tour

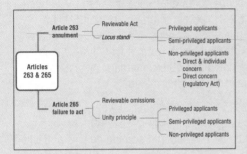

**Topic maps** – Visual guides highlight key subject areas and facilitate easy navigation through the chapter. Download them from the companion website to pin to your wall or add to your own revision notes.

**Revision checklist** – How well do you know each topic? Use these to identify essential points you should know for your exams. But don't panic if you don't know them all – the chapters will help you revise each point to ensure you are fully prepared for your exams. Print the checklists off the companion website and track your revision progress!

Revision checklist

**Essential points you should kno**

☐ The underlying purpose for judicia
☐ The Community Acts that can be a
☐ The Institutions that can be compe grounds for this
☐ The *locus standi* of an applicant
☐ The unity principle binding Art

**Sample questions** – Practice makes perfect! Read the question at the start of each chapter and consider how you would answer it. Guidance on structuring strong answers is provided at the end of the chapter. Try out additional sample questions online.

**Assessment advice** – Not sure how best to tackle a problem or essay question? Wondering what you may be asked? Be prepared – use the assessment advice to identify the ways in which a subject may be examined and how to apply your knowledge effectively.

**Don't be tempted to. . .** – Underlines areas where students most often trip up in exams. Use them to avoid making common mistakes and losing marks.

### ■ Sample question

Could you answer this question? Below is a typical essay question that could arise on this topic. Guidelines on answering the question are included at the end of this chapter, whilst a sample problem question and guidance on tackling it can be found on the companion website.

### ASSESSMENT ADVICE

**Essay questions** Essay questions in this area tend to focus upon some aspect of the judicial review mechanism. This can be, for example, the role this procedure has to play in the checks and balances system set up between the institutions; it can also be the difficulty which an individual faces in establishing *locus standi* and a discussion of the case law surrounding this issue.

**Problem questions** Problem questions, on the other hand, are more unusual, as they have to involve the creation of a scenario. This therefore can tend to focus upon the *locus standi* issue, as this will involve individuals.

### ! Don't be tempted to...

Don't think you can simply analogise Art. 265 with 263. The main problem here is that Art. 265 is even more restrictive than Art. 263, because it doesn't even allow applicants who have 'direct and individual concern' as Art. 263 does. The only individuals who can use Art. 265 are those to whom a decision *should* have been addressed.

**Make your answer stand out** – Illustrates sources of further thinking and debate where you can maximise your marks. Include these to really impress your examiners!

**KEY CASE**

Case 25/62 *Plaumann* v. *Commission* [1963] ECR 95

*Concerning: the test for individual concern*

**Facts**

This was a decision aimed at the German government instructing them to lift an import duty on clementines going into Germany. Plaumann claimed direct and individual concern.

✓ Make your answer stand out

Case C-309/89 *Codorniu* v. *EC Council* [1994] egal principle
whether Regulations with general application ey would be individually concerned if the decision affected them 'by reason of
Although normally any Act of general applica rtain attributes which are peculiar to them or by reason of circumstances in
individuals, in *Codorniu* the Regulation did h hich they are differentiated from all other persons'.
still be challenged because it had particular
bold move because the ECJ were saying th
applications at the same time. Unfortunat
enerally relaxing the rules, as it hasn't
e Treaty in this area do look like
*dorniu* though. A discus

**Key case and key statute boxes** – Identify the important elements of the essential cases and statutes you will need to know for your exams.

**KEY STATUTE**

**Article 263(4) TFEU**

Any natural or legal person may, under the conditions laid down in the first and second paragraphs, institute proceedings against an Act addressed to that person or which is of direct and individual concern to them, and against a regulatory Act which is of direct concern to them and does not entail implementing measures.

**Key definition boxes** – Make sure you understand essential legal terms. Use the flashcards online to test your recall!

**KEY DEFINITION: Reasoned opinion**

The reasoned opinion is a written statement from the Commission, which lays down the obligation concerned, and the reasons why the Member State has failed to meet this obligation. It should clearly spell out the Commission's objection, and therefore it should be possible for the Member State to know what it needs to do to rectify the problem.

**Glossary** – Forgotten the meaning of a word? This quick reference covers key definitions and other useful terms.

# Glossary of terms

The glossary is divided into two parts: key definitions and other useful terms. The key definitions can be found within the chapter in which they occur as well as here. These definitions are the essential terms that you must know and understand in order to prepare for an exam. The additional list of terms provides further definitions of useful terms and phrases which will also help you answer examination and coursework questions effectively. These terms are highlighted in the text as they occur but the definition can only be found here.

**Exam tips** – Feeling the pressure? These boxes indicate how you can improve your exam performance and your chances of getting those top marks!

**EXAM TIP**

The consequence of such strict requirements for non-privileged applicants is that very few actions may be brought by private individuals. This may seem to be rather harsh, however, when discussing this area, it is worth remembering that there are also important policy reasons for doing this. If the *locus standi* test were broader, then the consequence would likely be the clogging of the European courts with actions brought by those who aren't immediately affected by them.

**Revision notes** – Highlights related points or areas of overlap in other topics, or areas where your course might adopt a particular approach that you should check with your course tutor.

**REVISION NOTE**

Only secondary sources of law are dealt with by this area of the Treaty – Treaty Articles themselves cannot be challenged. See Chapter 2 for a fuller examination of those sources of law. In this chapter, where it refers to a 'Community Act', it concerns these secondary sources of law.

# Guided tour of the companion website

Book resources are available to download. Print your own **topic maps** and **revision checklists**!

Use the **study plan** prior to your revision to help you assess how well you know the subject and determine which areas need most attention. Choose to take the full assessment or focus on targeted study units.

'**Test your knowledge**' of individual areas with quizzes tailored specifically to each chapter. **Sample problem and essay questions** are also available with guidance on crafting a good answer.

**Flashcards** help improve recall of important legal terms and key cases and statutes. Available in both electronic and printable formats.

'**You be the marker**' gives you the chance to evaluate sample exam answers for different question types and understand how and why an examiner awards marks.

Download the **podcast** and listen as your own personal Law Express tutor guides you through a 10–15 minute audio session. You will be presented with a typical but challenging question and provided a step-by-step explanation on how to approach the question, what essential elements your answer will need for a pass, how to structure a good response, and what to do to make your answer stand out so that you can earn extra marks.

All of this and more can be found when you visit **www.pearsoned.co.uk/lawexpress**

# Table of cases and statutes

## ■ UK cases

## ■ EU cases

# ■ Statutes and EU legislation

# Directives

## Regulations

Regulation 1612/68/EEC **113, 117**
Regulation 1/2003/EC **128, 129, 135, 141, 142**

# ■ Conversion table for 2009 renumbering of the TFEU

Only Treaty Articles mentioned in this book are listed here. A more comprehensive list can be found in your main textbook, as well as on the Europa website – you can find a link on the *Law Express: EU Law* companion website or type the following into your web browser: http://eur-lex.europa.eu/LexUriServ/LexUriServ.do?uri=OJ:C:2008:115:0361:0388:EN:PDF

(Please note this requires Adobe Acrobat Reader.)

---

**REVISION NOTE**

The TFEU (commonly referred to as the Treaty of Rome) has been renumbered *twice* now. You need to be aware of this, as otherwise it may become confusing when looking at cases (particularly older ones) which refer to one of the two old numbering systems.

From the **1950s** through to the Treaty of Amsterdam (which came into force on **1 May 1999**), the original numbering system was used. Any cases between these times will refer to the original numbers of the Treaty of Rome.

The Amsterdam Treaty renumbered the original Treaty of Rome because with all the amendments that had occurred in over 50 years, the numbering had become untidy and complicated. This was effective from **May 1999** to **December 2009**.

On **1 December 2009**, the Lisbon Treaty renumbered the Treaty of Rome again, for much the same reason.

The table opposite gives all three versions of the Treaty numbers:

---

| Pre-Amsterdam numbering | Post-Amsterdam numbering | Post-Lisbon numbering |
|---|---|---|
| Article 137 EEC | Article 189 EC | Article 14 TEU |
| Article 5 EEC | Article 10 EC | Article 4(3) TEU |
| Article 9 EEC | Article 14 EC | Article 28 TFEU |
| Article 7 EEC | Article 15 EC | Article 29 TFEU |
| Article 12 EEC | Article 25 EC | Article 30 TFEU |
| Article 9 EEC | Article 23 EC | Article 31 TFEU |
| Article 7d EEC | Article 16 EC | Article 32 TFEU |
| Article 8a EEC | Article 18 EC | Article 33 TFEU |
| Article 30 EEC | Article 28 EC | Article 34 TFEU |
| Article 34 EEC | Article 29 EC | Article 35 TFEU |
| Article 36 EEC | Article 30 EC | Article 36 TFEU |
| Article 10 EEC | Article 24 EC | Article 37 TFEU |
| – | – | Article 39 TFEU |
| Article 57 EEC | Article 47 EC | Article 40 TFEU |
| Article 48 EEC | Article 39 EC | Article 45 TFEU |
| Article 49 EEC | Article 40 EC | Article 46 TFEU |
| Article 73m EEC | Article 65 EC | Article 81 TFEU |
| Article 85 EEC | Article 81 EC | Article 101 TFEU |
| Article 86 EEC | Article 82 EC | Article 102 TFEU |
| Article 138 EEC | Article 190 EC, paras 4 & 5 | Article 223 TFEU |
| Article 138a EEC | Article 191 EC, second para | Article 224 TFEU |
| Article 138b EEC | Article 192 EC, second para | Article 225 TFEU |
| Article 138c EEC | Article 193 EC | Article 226 TFEU |
| Article 138d EEC | Article 194 EC | Article 227 TFEU |
| Article 138e EEC | Article 195 EC | Article 228 TFEU |
| Article 139 EEC | Article 196 EC | Article 229 TFEU |
| Article 140 EEC | Article 197 EC, second, third and fourth paras | Article 230 TFEU |
| Article 141 EEC | Article 198 EC | Article 231 TFEU |
| Article 142 EEC | Article 199 EC | Article 232 TFEU |
| Article 143 EEC | Article 200 EC | Article 233 TFEU |

▶

| Pre-Amsterdam numbering | Post-Amsterdam numbering | Post-Lisbon numbering |
|---|---|---|
| Article 144 EEC | Article 201 EC | Article 234 TFEU |
| -- | -- | Article 235 TFEU |
| -- | -- | Article 236 TFEU |
| Article 147 EEC | Article 204 EC | Article 237 TFEU |
| Article 148 EEC | Article 205 EC, paras 1 & 3 | Article 238 TFEU |
| Article 150 EEC | Article 206 EC | Article 239 TFEU |
| Article 151 EEC | Article 207 EC | Article 240 TFEU |
| Article 152 EEC | Article 208 EC | Article 241 TFEU |
| Article 153 EEC | Article 209 EC | Article 242 TFEU |
| Article 154 EEC | Article 210 EC | Article 243 TFEU |
| -- | -- | Article 244 TFEU |
| Article 157 EEC | Article 213 EC | Article 245 TFEU |
| Article 159 EEC | Article 215 EC | Article 246 TFEU |
| Article 160 EEC | Article 216 EC | Article 247 TFEU |
| Article 161 EEC | Article 217 EC, para 2 | Article 248 TFEU |
| Article 162 EEC | Article 218 EC, para 2 | Article 249 TFEU |
| Article 163 EEC | Article 219 EC | Article 250 TFEU |
| Article 169 EEC | Article 226 EC | Article 258 TFEU |
| Article 170 EEC | Article 227 EC | Article 259 TFEU |
| Article 171 EEC | Article 228 EC | Article 260 TFEU |
| Article 173 EEC | Article 230 EC | Article 263 TFEU |
| Article 175 EEC | Article 232 EC | Article 265 TFEU |
| Article 177 EEC | Article 234 EC | Article 267 TFEU |
| Article 185 EEC | Article 242 EC | Article 278 TFEU |
| Article 186 EEC | Article 243 EC | Article 279 TFEU |
| Article 189 EEC | Article 249 EC | Article 288 TFEU |
| -- | -- | Article 289 TFEU |
| Article 189b | Article 251 EC | Article 294 TFEU |
| -- | -- | Article 15 TEU |
| -- | -- | Article 16 TEU |
| -- | -- | Article 17 TEU |

# Sources and application of EU law

**1**

# ■Topic map

# ◼ Introduction

## The operation of the EU is based upon its laws.

These laws are created either through amendments to the Treaties, or through the legislative powers given to the Institutions (see Chapter 2) and are, to a greater or lesser extent, enforceable in or against the countries of the EU.

The purpose of this chapter is to examine the sources of EU law, and to discuss the system under which they are enforceable. To this end, there are several main issues:

- The supremacy of EU law in Member States' jurisdictions
- The enforceability of those laws directly by individuals in national courts
- The difference between the ways in which those laws are treated

The EU is pretty unusual in international law. Normally it is very difficult to enforce laws upon signatory States of international agreements; however, the EU has built up a significant body of legislation and case law, referred to as the *acquis communitaire* – basically the existing law of the Community. States can be held to account for non-implementation (this is dealt with in Chapter 3) and individuals in certain situations can directly enforce rights given to them under EU law.

## ASSESSMENT ADVICE

This area is very broad, and therefore there is a wide range of assessment questions which could be asked regarding sources of law. These may range from problem questions concerning direct effects through to essay questions on the supremacy of EU law. All these questions have one thing in common – they concern the way in which EU law affects the law of Member States; in particular, the UK.

This is an area of law that has been developed through the case law. It is very important to make sure you are familiar with the key cases that have developed the law here. Examiners will not mark you very highly if you cannot demonstrate a good knowledge of relevant key cases: this chapter will highlight a lot of them.

# ■ Sample question

Could you answer this question? Below is a typical essay question that could arise on this topic. Guidelines on answering the question are included at the end of this chapter, whilst a sample problem question and guidance on tackling it can be found on the companion website.

---

## ESSAY QUESTION

'It is true that by Article 189 [then 249, now Art. 288] regulations are directly applicable and may therefore certainly produce direct effects by virtue of their nature as law. However, it does not follow from this that other categories of legal measures mentioned in that Article could never produce similar effects.'

Case 9/70 *Franz Grad* v. *Finanzamt Traustein* [1970] ECR 825 at 837

Discuss.

---

# ■ Forms of EU legislation

EU law falls broadly into two categories, **primary legislation** and **secondary legislation**:

- Primary legislation comes from the Treaties
- Secondary legislation comes from the law-making powers given to the Institutions under Art. 288

## Primary legislation

> **!** Don't be tempted to...
>
> Take care not to confuse the different Treaties with each other. There are now a range of Treaties that affect EU law. However, their place is easy to understand, as follows:
>
> - The Treaty of Rome is the founding Treaty of the European Economic Community (now European Union) and is the main Treaty to refer to. Where this book refers to 'the Treaty', then it is this Treaty which is meant. The Treaty of Lisbon has changed the name of this Treaty, and it is now referred to as the Treaty on the Functioning of the European Union (TFEU)
>
> - The Single European Act, Maastricht Treaty (Treaty on European Union), Amsterdam Treaty, Treaty of Nice and Lisbon Treaty have all amended the

Treaty of Rome, and therefore usually you will not need to refer to them directly (with the exception of the Maastricht Treaty which was a more significant amendment than others). Any changes these Treaties have made are included in the most up-to-date version of the Treaty of Rome on the Europa website: http://europa.eu/

■ Please bear in mind that the Treaty on European Union has now been given greater significance by the changes made by the Lisbon Treaty, and therefore the TFEU is no longer the only Treaty to which you will commonly need to refer.

The order of the Treaties is given in the following table.

| Signed | In force from | Treaty |
| --- | --- | --- |
| 1957 | 1 January 1958 | Treaty of Rome – EC Treaty |
| 1986 | 1 July 1987 | Single European Act |
| 1992 | 1 November 1993 | Treaty of Maastricht (Treaty on European Union) |
| 1997 | 1 May 1999 | Treaty of Amsterdam |
| 1999 | 1 February 2003 | Treaty of Nice |
| 2007 | 1 December 2009 | Treaty of Lisbon |

Primary legislation is only made when Member States meet and agree amendments; usually at intergovernmental conferences. The laws contained in Treaties cannot be changed in any other way, and must do so with the agreement of all Member States. This is why often there is a considerable delay before a Treaty comes into force – the Lisbon Treaty demonstrates the political problems that can be encountered when bringing out a new Treaty.

The Constitutional Treaty is not included in this list because it was never completely ratified. France and Holland voted against this Treaty in referenda held after its signature in 2004, and so it never became part of EU law.

## Secondary legislation

Secondary legislation is made by the Institutions under the powers given to them by Art. 288.

**Article 288(1) TFEU**

To exercise the Union's competences, the institutions shall adopt regulations, directives, decisions, recommendations and opinions.

The five different forms of secondary legislation can be defined as follows:

| Form of legislation | Effect |
| --- | --- |
| Regulations (Article 288(2)) | Generally applicable – automatically become law in all Member States |
| Directives (Article 288(3)) | Applicable to all Member States, but require some form of enabling legislation from national parliaments of Member States |
| Decisions (Article 288(4)) | Binding only on those parties to whom they are addressed |
| Recommendations and Opinions (Article 288(5)) | Non-binding Acts |

# ■ Supremacy of EU law

Nowhere in the Treaties themselves is there any reference to the supremacy of EU law, or its hierarchy with the national laws of the Member States. Instead this principle has evolved from case law of the European Court of Justice (ECJ).

**Case 6/64 *Costa* v. *ENEL* [1964] ECR 585**

*Concerning: supremacy of EU Law*

**Facts**

This case concerned a conflict between several Treaty provisions and an Italian statute which nationalised the electricity company in Italy.

**Legal principle**

The ECJ said: 'By creating a Community of unlimited duration, having its own institutions, its own personality, its own legal capacity and capacity of representation on the international plane and, more particularly, real powers stemming from a limitation of sovereignty or a transfer of powers from the States of the Community [i.e. Union], the Member States have limited their sovereign rights, albeit within limited fields, and have thus created a body of law which binds both their nationals and themselves.' This therefore established that the Member States had agreed to prioritise EU law above their own within certain areas.

This was also followed by Case 11/70 *International Handelsgesellschaft mbH* [1970] ECR 1125, which went further than *Costa* v. *ENEL* by stating that even secondary EU law (in that case a Regulation) was a higher form of law than the constitution of a Member State. Although this would not affect the UK, as currently there is no written constitution, it does have significance in most of the other EU Member States, as they do.

When a Member State joins the EU, they effectively agree to be bound by its laws (as confirmed by *Costa* v. *ENEL*, above), both primary and secondary. In particular, Art. 4(3) of the Treaty on European Union imposes a general obligation on all Member States to make sure they fulfil all obligations under the Treaty. (Until the Lisbon amendments, this was Art. 10 of the Treaty of Rome.) This created a problem with the UK constitutional system when the UK joined in 1972, as the UK system is **dualist**.

**KEY DEFINITION: Dualist**

A legal system where any international agreements signed by that State's government can only become law when legislation is enacted in that country to ratify that agreement. This is common in systems where the parliament is supreme, like the UK constitutional system. This is the opposite of monist systems, where any international agreement automatically becomes part of that State's law merely because the government has signed it.

# The doctrine of parliamentary supremacy

The doctrine of parliamentary supremacy creates problems, because it states that:

■ Parliament is the highest law-making body in the UK
■ No other law can override the wishes of Parliament
■ Parliament cannot bind its successors

The first of these issues was addressed because when the UK joined the EU (at that time the EEC), Parliament enacted the European Communities Act 1972.

**KEY STATUTE**

### European Communities Act 1972, s.2(1)

All rights, powers, liabilities, obligations and restrictions ... arising ... under ... the Treaties are without further enactment to be given legal effect or used in the United Kingdom and shall be recognised and available in law, and be enforced, allowed and followed accordingly ...

Therefore the EU Treaties are recognised as part of UK law because of the European Communities Act, and so this should deal with the issue created by the doctrine of parliamentary supremacy. The thing to note specifically from this case is that the Treaties are adopted into UK law 'without further enactment' and therefore this deals with all other Treaties that may be ratified by the UK as well. What it didn't do was deal with the other two bullet points above, concerning overriding laws and binding successors. These issues were debated in the courts shortly after the UK joined the EU. It created uncertainty at the time, because the judiciary were unused to having to deal with EU law as well as UK law. The rules that evolved at that time have therefore established how the UK courts deal with EU laws.

# Dealing with inconsistent laws

Joining the EU therefore had two consequences for the UK:

- Any existing national laws inconsistent with EU laws must be repealed
- The Member State must not enact laws in the future which are inconsistent with EU law

The first of these was probably more straightforward to deal with, as the enactment of the European Communities Act could be seen as an indication from Parliament that they agreed to remove previous inconsistent laws. The second consequence was more difficult to deal with.

First, let's look at why EU law was regarded as supreme. The Treaty itself does not make any mention about EU law being supreme, but this is an issue which has been discussed repeatedly by the ECJ, and the *Costa* case mentioned above is probably the best example. Also, in Case 26/62 *Van Gend en Loos* v. *Nederlandse Administratie der Belastingen* [1963] ECR 1, the ECJ said: '... the Community constitutes a new legal order in international law, for whose benefit the States have limited their sovereign rights ...' and therefore limited their ability to make laws which go against the Treaty. The significance of this was discussed by Lord Denning in the following case.

**KEY CASE**

*Macarthys* v. *Smith* [1979] 3 All ER 325

*Concerning: The effect of the EC Treaty on the application of UK law in the courts*

**Facts**

This case involved a claim by a women for equal pay with a male counterpart. The Equal Pay Act 1970 would not have given her a remedy, however Art. 141 of the EEC Treaty (as it was then) would have. The court had to decide whether the law under the Treaty gave her a right that she could enforce directly.

**Legal principle**

Lord Denning said:

> In construing our statute, we are entitled to look at the treaty as an aid to its construction: and even more, not only as an aid but as an overriding force. If on close investigation it should appear that our legislation is deficient – or is inconsistent with Community law – by some oversight of our draftsmen – then it is our bounden duty to give priority to Community law.

This is fine where the statute concerned can be reinterpreted, and this in fact forms the basis of indirect effect (see later in this chapter for details) but the principle here was properly tested in the next case, where there appeared to have been a deliberate attempt to go against EU law by enacting a conflicting UK law.

**KEY CASE**

*R* v. *Secretary of State for Transport, ex parte Factortame (No. 2)* [1990] 3 CMLR 1

*Concerning: supremacy of EU law and conflicting national law*

**Facts**

A dispute arose over the Merchant Shipping Act 1988, which attempted to restrict ownership of UK registered fishing boats by requiring that at least 75 per cent of the boat must be owned by UK nationals. The courts had to decide, as there was a direct conflict between the Merchant Shipping Act and the EC Treaty, which should be applied.

**Legal principle**

After referring this to the ECJ for clarification, the House of Lords decided that where there is conflict between a national law and Community law, that the doctrine of parliamentary supremacy is modified by s.2(4) of the European Communities Act 1972, and allowed the House of Lords to disregard the Merchant Shipping ▶

Act, something it had never been able to do before. In this case, this allowed the Spanish fishermen who complained to the courts to get interim relief, and eventually led to the relevant parts of the Merchant Shipping Act being repealed.

It is important to point out that this is the case *regardless of whether the Act in question came before or after the European Communities Act.*

As a consequence, the European Communities Act appears to give the TFEU a kind of higher status. There is implied in the situation set by the cases the idea that no matter what UK law is inconsistent with EU law, that the Treaty will still have priority.

# ■ Direct applicability and direct effects

So EU law is supreme, however when applying it to real situations (as, for example, when you are asked to apply the law to problem-based scenarios), then you also need to be able to show whether it can be directly used or not. This is where the concepts of direct applicability and direct effects come in. Being able to use these concepts will enable you to say whether someone can use an EU law in their national court or not.

**! Don't be tempted to...**

There is often confusion between the terms *direct applicability* and *direct effect*. It is important not to get these two concepts mixed up as they are quite different. As a general definition, you can think of the two as follows:

**Direct applicability**: EU law is directly applicable if it is recognised as part of UK law. Treaties and Regulations are directly applicable because they become part of UK law as a result of the European Communities Act 1972. Directives are not directly applicable as they need an implementing piece of UK legislation to become law in the UK.

**Directly effective**: EU law is directly effective if it can be enforced in a UK court. There are two types of direct effects, horizontal and vertical. The difference between these is explained further below.

Linked to the issue of supremacy of Community law is the question of directly enforcing Community law in national courts. The above discussion has shown that Community law overrides UK law, but this is meaningless unless a person can enforce those laws in a UK court. However, in certain circumstances, Community law has been held to be directly enforceable in national courts through the doctrine of direct effects. This was first raised in the following key case.

**KEY CASE**

Case 26/62 *Van Gend en Loos* v. *Nederlandse Administratie der Belastingen* [1963] ECR 1

*Concerning: direct effect of Community law in national courts*

**Facts**

This case concerned Art. 30 (at that time Art. 12, then subsequently Art. 25 pre-Lisbon) of the Treaty which prohibited new customs duties being imposed, or existing customs duties being increased. Through a case in the Dutch courts, Van Gend was trying to directly enforce the rule in Art. 30 against the Dutch government, claiming it gave them a right not to be taxed in this way. The question was referred to the ECJ under Art. 267 (at that time 177).

**Legal principle**

Although Art. 30 was a prohibition, the ECJ said that Van Gend could enforce this against the Dutch government if the following criteria were fulfilled:

■ That it was a clear and unconditional prohibition
■ That it imposed a duty without any discretion given to the Member States
■ That it produced direct effects between Member States and citizens.

As these criteria were fulfilled in this case, then the national court could enforce Art. 30 in favour of Van Gend.

**KEY CASE**

Case 41/74 *Van Duyn* v. *Home Office* [1974] ECR 1337

*Concerning: criteria for establishing whether a provision of Community law has direct effect*

**Facts**

The UK government was attempting to exclude Van Duyn, a Dutch national, from the UK because of her membership of an 'undesirable' organisation, the Church of Scientology. Part of this case looked at whether Directive 64/221 could be directly enforced by Van Duyn.

**Legal principle**

In order for a provision of Community law to have direct effects, it must be:

■ Clear and precise
■ Unconditional/without exceptions
■ Not require any implementation by the Member States

These cases clearly established that it was possible for an individual to enforce a rule of Community law, without having to rely upon a national rule, despite the fact that this was usually required as Directives are specifically implemented individually by the Member States. The application of this rule, however, will be different according to the different type of Community Act being enforced. Treaties and Regulations are directly applicable and directly effective, but Directives are not directly applicable, and are only directly **effective vertically**.

# Vertical and horizontal effect

**KEY DEFINITION: Vertical and horizontal effect**

A Community law is **vertically effective** when it is enforceable only against the State. It is **horizontally effective** when it is enforceable against private individuals (people and companies) as well as against the State.

| Type of community law | Vertically/horizontally effective? |
|---|---|
| Treaties | Can be both vertically and **horizontally effective**, depending on the nature of the right being given by the Treaty article – you need to refer to *Van Gend en Loos* |
| Regulations | Can be both vertically and horizontally effective |
| Directives | Vertically effective only – a Directive is an instruction to a State to introduce a law into their own legal system |
| Decisions | Decisions are addressed to particular parties – so they are enforceable only against those parties |

# The problem of direct effect of Directives

This is the part of direct effect that students struggle with most – directly enforcing a Directive in a national court causes the most problems because of the nature of a Directive. Directives are instructions to the Member States to enact a law, and therefore they are only capable of having vertical effect. The main thing to note is that Directives do not *automatically* have direct effects, and so if a person wants to enforce them in a national court, they must make sure the following conditions apply.

| Condition | Case example |
|---|---|
| The Directive must give clearly identifiable rights to individuals | Case 43/75 *Defrenne* v. *SABENA (No. 2)* [1979] ECR 1365 |
| The time limit for the Member State to implement the Directive must have passed | Case 148/78 *Pubblico Ministero* v. *Ratti* [1979] ECR 1629 |
| The Directive can be enforced only against the State (vertically) | Case 152/84 *Marshall* v. *Southampton & South West Hampshire Area Health Authority* [1986] ECR 723 |

## ! Don't be tempted to...

One area where the ECJ has been flexible with its definition concerns the meaning of 'the State' under the vertical effects rule. This is an area where students can be caught out when dealing with a problem question which involves vertical effect. Look at these three examples:

- In Case C-188/89 *Foster* v. *British Gas* [1990] ECR I-3313 the ECJ said that a body would be part of the State if it:
  - is subject to the control of the State
  - has special powers given to it by the State

- Case 152/84 *Marshall* v. *Southampton & South West Hampshire Area Health Authority* [1986] ECR 723 shows that 'the State' is 'the State' regardless of what function it is performing (in *Marshall* it was acting as an employer)

- In *NUT* v. *Governing Body of St. Mary's Church of England (Aided) Junior School* [1997] 3 CMLR 630 the court decided that the definition of 'the State' should be a 'broad one'. Schools and other educational establishments would therefore be part of 'the State'

When thinking about whether something is part of 'the State', it is important to bear in mind this broad definition – but there are limits: see *Rolls Royce* v. *Doughty* [1992] ICR 538 where, although Rolls Royce were publicly owned, they were not part of 'the State' as they did not fulfil the other criteria associated with being part of 'the State' (see above).

# ■ Other ways of enforcing EU law in national courts

## Indirect effect

When EU law imposes an obligation on 'the State', the definition is very broad, and therefore also includes the courts as well. This has led to the ECJ finding that the courts also have an obligation to interpret national law in line with EU law.

---

**KEY CASE**

### Case 14/83 *von Colson* v. *Land Nordrhein-Westfalen* [1984] ECR 1891

*Concerning: Indirect effect of Community law*

**Facts**

This case involved two female social workers who were attempting to claim rights under the Equal Treatment Directive. They could not claim rights directly under the Directive, however the ECJ decided that the Directive could still be useful through what became indirect effect.

**Legal principle**

The ECJ developed what is often referred to as the 'von Colson principle': that as national courts are part of the State, they are under an obligation to interpret national law in line with Community law. This can mean that an individual can enforce a law from the EU against another individual in a national court.

---

This appears to solve all problems created by the limits of direct effects (particularly with Directives, because they can only have vertical effects), but if you look at Case C-106/89 *Marleasing* v. *La Comercial Internacional de Alimentación* [1990] ECR I-4135, it is important that a national law *exists* that can be interpreted.

Below is an example of how it has been dealt with by judges in the UK.

---

**KEY CASE**

### *Litster* v. *Forth Dry Dock* [1989] 2 WLR 634

*Concerning: the application of indirect effect in the UK*

**Facts**

This concerned Directive 77/187, which was intended to protect workers who were dismissed as a result of a transfer of a business. The UK statutory

---

instrument that enacted it required that workers dismissed immediately before the transfer should be protected. The employees in question were dismissed one hour before the transfer, and so on a literal interpretation were not employed immediately before the transfer.

### Legal principle

The House of Lords (now the Supreme Court) decided that they had to construe the UK Regulations in such a way that it 'accords with the decisions of the European Court upon the corresponding provisions of the Directive to which the Regulation was intended to give effect'. They interpreted the Regulations so that those employees dismissed one hour before transfer were protected, as this was consistent with the wording of the Directive.

## State liability for non-implementation

There is one final method of gaining a remedy based on EU law – to sue the State because of its failure to implement a piece of legislation where it was obliged to do so. This is *mainly* relevant to Directives, because they normally need a national law to give effect to them, but not exclusively.

### KEY CASE

### Case C-6&9/90 *Francovich* v. *Italy* [1991] ECR I-5357

*Concerning: state liability for failing to implement a Directive*

### Facts

This case concerned employees of a bankrupt company who were trying to claim wages arrears, something which was guaranteed by a Directive which Italy had failed to implement. Because they could not sue their former employer (because that would have involved a horizontal effect, not possible with a Directive) they then sued the Italian State, claiming that it was at fault because they could not get a remedy.

### Legal principle

The ECJ held that the Italian State would be liable for their failure to implement the Directive if the following three conditions were fulfilled:

- The Directive gave rights to individuals
- Those rights were identifiable within the wording of the Directive
- There was a causal link between the failure to implement and the damage caused to the individual

This has now been applied to all forms of Community law (see Cases C-46&48/93 *Brasserie du Pecheur* v. *Germany* and *R* v. *Secretary of State for Transport, ex parte Factortame* [1996] ECR I-1029). These cases also added the requirement that the breach must be 'sufficiently serious' in order to be able to apply this principle to all forms of Community law.

 **Make your answer stand out**

A more controversial aspect of State liability has been the idea that the State could be liable for the actions of the judiciary. This does fit in with the broader concept of 'the State' as discussed by the ECJ. This is controversial because the State does not have any control or influence over the judiciary. If you encounter a question where the judiciary are breaching EU law, or are required to fulfil obligations under Art. 4(3) TEU, then you might consider this point. See Anagnostaras (2001).

## The problem of non-implementation of Directives and the post-Lisbon solution

Many problems have been encountered in the past where a State has failed to implement a Directive and therefore an individual has not been able to get a remedy. This is where the rule of vertical effect for Directives creates an unfair split between the public and the private sectors, because although those in the public sector may be able to argue that they are suing an 'emanation of the State' under the principles in *Foster* v. *British Gas*, those who may need to enforce Directives against private bodies will be unfairly prejudiced. A mechanism to minimise this is in the new Art. 260 (formerly 228). The Commission can recommend a fine the *first* time the matter goes to the ECJ when the infringement by the State is about failing to comply with EU law, and not have to wait for a second action. The aim is to deter States from attempting to use the long Art. 258 procedure to avoid enacting Directives.

# ■ **Chapter summary**: putting it all together

## Test yourself

- ☐ Can you tick all the points from the **revision checklist** at the beginning of this chapter?
- ☐ Attempt the **sample question** from the beginning of this chapter using the answer guidelines below.

☐ Go to the **companion website** to access more revision support online, including interactive quizzes, sample questions with answer guidelines, 'you be the marker' exercises, flashcards and podcasts you can download.

# Answer guidelines

See the essay question at the start of the chapter.

## Approaching the question

This question is focused upon the principle of direct effects discussed in part of this chapter, but it is also broad enough to enable you to bring in other areas of this topic from this chapter. You need to discuss Art. 288 and the way that direct effect has affected the application of the types of laws discussed.

## Important points to include

- In your answer, you will need to address the following:
- The distinction between direct applicability and direct effect
- The different rules for direct applicability/effect of Treaties, Regulations, Directives, Decisions
- A discussion of how the rules have been applied by the courts to these different forms of legislation; in particular, the way in which rules concerning Directives have evolved
- How the shortcomings of direct effect of Directives (lack of horizontal effect) have been addressed through use of indirect effect and state liability for non-implementation

### ✓ Make your answer stand out

This question is asking you to explain the operation of the rules of direct applicability/effect to forms of legislation other than Regulations, and the most complicated of these is Directives. Directives create problems because of the nature of what they are: instructions to Member States. Therefore if you can show your appreciation of the limitations of Directives, and how the courts have developed rules to deal with this (for example, the broad definition of 'the State' discussed above) as well as the limitations still in existence (the ▶

difference in employees in the public and private sectors under the rules in *Marshall*, for example) then you can demonstrate an understanding of how these rules work in practice.

## READ TO IMPRESS

Anagnostaras, G. (2001) The Principle of State Liability for Judicial Breaches: The Impact of European Community Law, 7 EPL 281

Craig, P. (1991) Sovereignty of the United Kingdom Parliament after *Factortame*, 9 YEL 221

Craig, P. (1997) Directives: Direct Effect, Indirect Effect and the Construction of National Legislation, 22 EL Rev 519

Craig, P. (1997) Once More Unto the Breach: The Community, the State and Damages Liability, 113 LQR 67

Steiner, J. (1993) From Direct Effects to *Francovich*: Shifting Means of Enforcement of Community Law, 18 EL Rev 3

Tridimas, T. (2002) Black, White, and Shades of Grey: Horizontality of Directives Revisited, 21 YEL 327

## NOTES

# The Institutions of the EU and the decision-making process

2

## Revision checklist

**Essential points you should know:**

- [ ] The structure of the EU Institutions and how they relate to each other
- [ ] The role of each of the Institutions, and their powers and duties
- [ ] How the above affects both the political and legal life of the Community, and the implications of the exercise of those powers by the Institutions

# ■ Topic map

# ■Introduction

## The EU is run by its Institutions.

The key to understanding the way in which the EU operates, therefore, lies in understanding the functions of the Institutions. The EU has two very important roles which have a very real effect on the Member States. First, it makes law, whether that be through Treaties or secondary legislation, and secondly, it provides adjudication on those laws applicable to all Member States. Each of the Institutions has a key role in achieving these functions, and their powers and their interrelationships are important in showing how this works. The functions and powers of the Institutions tend not to contribute to their own discrete question in an examination, as something focused purely on the mechanics of how the Institutions do things would present a topic purely descriptive in nature. However, an analysis of the politics of how the Institutions work and the political context in which EU law operates can form part of a question in this area. It also helps to understand the Institutions for other topics such as the legislative process itself, and the actions of the three main Institutions when appearing in front of the ECJ. This is why this chapter covers both of these areas which, you may have noticed, are dealt with discretely in most textbooks. There is often one chapter describing the Institutions, and one describing their roles and powers. However, we are going to examine the relationships between the Institutions alongside the information about who they are, in order to understand how the powers of each Institution interrelate, and in order for you to understand how this information is relevant and applicable in an examination situation.

One further thing to bear in mind – with the reforms from the Lisbon Treaty, the Institutional structure is one thing which has changed in such a way that it affects how you analyse the relationships between the Institutions. You therefore need to be careful about using out-of-date information and older textbooks. For example, the European Council now has status as a Treaty institution, which it didn't have before.

## ASSESSMENT ADVICE

**Essay questions** In this area of European Law essay questions will commonly focus on some aspect of the relationship between two or more of the institutions. Such questions will usually require you to have the knowledge of the functions of the Institutions, but will also require you to use that knowledge to analyse the relationships between the Institutions concerned. So you must remember that this is not an exercise in memorising large quantities of factual information, and will require some form of critique on your part.

**Problem questions** Questions covering this area will generally be ones which overlap with other areas of EU law, for example relating to an aspect of an Institution's powers, like the Commission's power of enforcement under Art. 258. You will need to understand how the Institutions work in order to advise how the procedures might affect your answer to the question.

# ■ Sample question

Could you answer this question? Below is a typical essay question that could arise on this topic. Guidelines on answering the question are included at the end of this chapter, whilst a sample problem question and guidance on tackling it can be found on the companion website.

### ESSAY QUESTION

'... it has become common to speak of an 'institutional balance' within Community institutions, and the way in which this is evoked draws on a system of checks and balances not dissimilar to those we find in more traditional governmental systems. The EU institutions have come to operate a system of checks on each other, sometimes referred to in the context of an "institutional balance" ...'

Douglass-Scott, S., *Constitutional Law of the European Union* (Longman, 2002), Chapter 2 at p. 49)

To what extent does the above statement apply to the current relationship between the Commission, the Council of Ministers, the European Council and the European Parliament, particularly as regards maintaining the balance of interests between the European Union and the Member States?

# ■ The Institutions of the EU

The three primary *legislative* Institutions (Figure 2.1) exist to represent different parties in the EU:

■ The Council of Ministers represents the interests of the Member States' governments

■ The European Parliament serves the interests of the EU citizens, and

■ The Commission's role is to serve the interests of the EU as an organisation

**Figure 2.1**

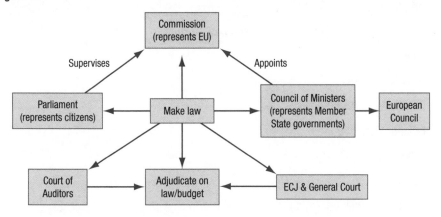

Additionally, the European Court of Justice (ECJ) and Court of First Instance (CFI) are there to adjudicate on cases arising from the Treaty, and there are also other Institutions which serve in an advisory or consultative role, such as the Economic and Social Committee, or the Committee of the Regions.

# ■ Composition of the Institutions

## The European Parliament

The European Parliament is constituted of 736 MEPs directly elected by individual citizens of the EU in elections. The number of MEPs allocated to a Member State varies according to population size, with Germany as the state with the largest population size having the largest number of MEPs (99) and Malta, as the state with the smallest population, having just 5. The division is criticised because it is not even – a German MEP will represent a larger number of citizens than an MEP from Luxembourg. The exact numbers after the January 2007 expansion are as follows:

| State | No. of MEPs per State |
| --- | --- |
| Germany | 99 |
| France, UK, Italy | 72 |
| Poland, Spain | 50 |
| Holland | 25 |
| Romania | 33 |

| State | No. of MEPs per State |
| --- | --- |
| Belgium, Czech Republic, Greece, Hungary, Portugal | 22 |
| Sweden | 18 |
| Bulgaria, Austria | 17 |
| Denmark, Finland, Slovakia | 13 |
| Ireland, Lithuania | 12 |
| Latvia | 8 |
| Slovenia | 7 |
| Cyprus, Estonia, Luxembourg | 6 |
| Malta | 5 |

Currently MEPs are only organised according to national party divisions, and are elected for a period of 5 years. There is a cap of 750 currently in place, to deal with any additional countries that may join. If several new countries join, then there may need to be a reduction in the number of MEPs for each State (as there was in 2004).

## Why is this important?

The European Parliament is directly elected by the population of the EU. Although the MEPs will inevitably be connected with the national parties in each of the States, they are not an extension of the government there. And as the MEPs come from all the political parties in a particular State, they do not represent the interests of the government of the day. Because of this, they are primarily there to represent the interests of the people in their constituency. They are directly linked to the citizens of the EU.

 Make your answer stand out

The development of the European Parliament from the point that direct elections were introduced is an important theme in EU law. It has a significant effect on the balance between the Institutions, and remembering this will help you in your discussion about the relationships between them. Increasing powers have been given to the European Parliament over the years because it is democratic (at least it is perceived as such as it is the only body where people are directly elected to it), and a direct link to EU citizens. The EU has shown that it believes that increasing its powers addresses the problems of 'democratic deficit' (discussed later in this chapter).

# The Council of the European Union (commonly, the Council of Ministers)

The Council of Ministers is composed of ministerial representatives of the Member State governments. Each State will send a minister relevant to the matter being debated, and therefore the representative will vary accordingly. There used to be as many as 22 configurations, but this has now been reduced to 9 (listed below). You can see the types of issues covered by discussions in the Council.

- General Affairs and External Relations
- Economic and Financial Affairs
- Competitiveness
- Cooperation in the fields of Justice and Home Affairs
- Transport, Telecommunications and Energy
- Agriculture and Fisheries
- Environment
- Education, Youth and Culture

Each State has a number of votes, and the votes are weighted in a similar way to the weighting in the European Parliament.

| State | Number of votes in the Council of Ministers |
|---|---|
| Germany, France, Italy, UK | 29 |
| Spain, Poland | 27 |
| Romania | 14 |
| Holland | 13 |
| Belgium, Czech Republic, Greece, Hungary, Portugal | 12 |
| Austria, Bulgaria, Sweden | 10 |
| Denmark, Ireland, Lithuania, Slovakia, Finland | 7 |
| Estonia, Cyprus, Latvia, Luxembourg, Slovenia | 4 |
| Malta | 3 |

This makes a total of 345 votes. The Council of Ministers will vote either by **qualified majority voting**, bare majority, or unanimity.

**KEY DEFINITION: Qualified majority voting**

Qualified majority voting (QMV) requires the following:

- A minimum of 255 out of 345 votes cast in favour
- A majority of all Member States voting in favour
- At least 62% of the EU's total population represented by the vote in favour

Voting can be a complicated and highly political issue. Type in the following link in your computer's web browser to go to the EU's own 'Voting Calculator' at http://www.consilium.europa.eu/App/calculette/default.aspx?lang=en&cmsid=1690

# Presidency of the Council of Ministers

Under the previous system, the Presidency of the Council of Ministers was held by each of the Member States in turn, for a period of 6 months. During that time, the State which held the Presidency put forward proposals and reforms that they wanted to implement, and proposed policies they favoured. The head of government for that State represented the State as President of the Council of Ministers. Prior to the introduction of the Lisbon Treaty, the Presidency was seen as significant in terms of the strategic discussions on the policies of the EU by heads of state of Member countries. However, this is now replaced under the Lisbon reforms with 'team presidencies', and each of the configurations listed above would have a Member State in charge, with the exception of the Foreign Affairs configuration. These would be rotated in the same way as before.

**! Don't be tempted to...**

With the introduction of the new Lisbon Treaty in December 2009, the European Council is now an official Institution of the EU. However, it is important not to confuse it with the Council of Ministers, as they have very different roles to play. The European Council arose from unofficial meetings of the heads of state of the Member States, and its main purpose is to discuss the policy direction of the EU.

# European Council

The European Council is now an official Institution of the EU. It is easily confused with the Council of Ministers, as they are both made up of representatives of national governments. However, they each has a different role to play. Put simply:

- The Council of Ministers' role is broadly stated, under Art. 16 TEU, to coordinate the economic policies of the Member States, and to take decisions. They are involved in making legislation and in the running of the EU. Their powers can also be found in Arts. 237–243 TFEU

- The European Council's responsibilities are described in Art. 15 TEU as being to 'provide the Union with the necessary impetus for its development and shall define the general political directions and priorities thereof. It shall not exercise legislative functions'

## The President of the European Council

The Lisbon Treaty has introduced a new office – that of President of the European Council. This office replaces the revolving 6-monthly presidency system previously operated, and is a post elected by qualified majority of the Member States (see Art. 15(5) and (6) TEU). The office runs for 2½ years, and can only be renewed once. In December 2009, the first President of the European Council was appointed, Herman Van Rumpuy. Before taking this office, he had been the Belgian Prime Minister. The overall responsibility of the President is contained in Art. 15(6) TEU:

**KEY STATUTE**

### Article 15(6) TEU

The President of the European Council:

(a) shall chair it and drive forward its work;
(b) shall ensure the preparation and continuity of the work of the European Council in cooperation with the President of the Commission, and on the basis of the work of the General Affairs Council;
(c) shall endeavour to facilitate cohesion and consensus within the European Council;
(d) shall present a report to the European Parliament after each of the meetings of the European Council.

The President of the European Council shall, at his level and in that capacity, ensure the external representation of the Union on issues concerning its common foreign and security policy, without prejudice to the powers of the High Representative of the Union for Foreign Affairs and Security Policy.

The President of the European Council shall not hold a national office.

**EXAM TIP**

The new office of President of the European Council, along with the post of High Representative for Foreign Affairs and Security Policy and the recognition of the European Council as a Treaty Institution, marks a significant change in the structure of the EU. If you encounter a question which asks you to comment on these developments, or generally about the direction of the EU (for example, an examiner might ask a general question about federalism), then you should be critically reviewing these developments as part of your answer.

## European Commission

The European Commission consists of one appointed Commissioner from each State. Each Commissioner will represent a different area of the Commission's business, for example trade and industry or the environment, known as a portfolio. They will also be supported by Directorates General. The President of the Commission will also choose a number of Vice-Presidents – although there is theoretically no limit to the number that can be appointed.

**EXAM TIP**

Where examination questions focus upon the Institutions, you should not use this as an opportunity to merely regurgitate facts about their composition and powers. The study of the Institutions is as much about the intricacies of how they allow the EU to function as it is about their powers. For example, the fact that the Commission is constituted of a representative of each State goes a long way towards helping the Member States to feel involved in policy-making, and to accept policies coming out of the Commission, despite the fact that Commissioners are persons 'whose independence is beyond doubt' – Art. 245 TFEU.

## The European Court of Justice and the General Court

**REVISION NOTE**

Although it is important to know what the ECJ and the General Court are, you will tend to find assessment questions will more readily concentrate on what they *do*, and how this affects the operation of the EU. For example, see Chapter 5 on the Art. 267 reference procedure, or Chapters 3 and 4 on the contentious procedures that take place in the ECJ and the General Court.

**!** Don't be tempted to...

Don't confuse the courts of the EU with any other 'European' courts. Remember when European courts are mentioned here, that these are the EU's own courts, and they are given the role of dealing with the laws of the EU. You should not, for example, confuse the European Court of Justice (ECJ) with the European Court of Human Rights (ECHR) as this is an entirely separate court, dealing with entirely different matters, and not part of the EU structure.

## Other Institutions

There are also several other Institutions involved in the day-to-day processes of the EU, shown in the following table.

| Institution | Role | Personnel |
| --- | --- | --- |
| Economic and Social Committee | To be consulted by the Council and Commission on legislative proposals<br><br>Can also submit their own opinion on European matters without being asked | Representatives of various groups concerned with economic activities, such as manufacturers, farmers, trade unionists, or public interest groups |
| Committee of the Regions | To be consulted by the Council and Commission on legislative proposals | Representatives of regional interests |
| Court of Auditors | To control and supervise the implementation of the budget | One member from each of the 27 Member States |

## ■ Powers of the Institutions

The powers of the primary Institutions can be broadly broken down into **legislative and supervisory power**, and it is a combination of these two types of power that helps with the smooth running of the EU.

**Legislative power** The involvement of an Institution in amending, or agreeing to, legislation made by the EU under the EC Treaty.

**Supervisory power** The power of an Institution to monitor, supervise or scrutinise the actions of another Institution in the EU Institutional structure.

| Institution | Powers and duties |
| --- | --- |
| European Parliament (see Art. 14 TEU and Arts. 223–234 TFEU) | Participates in the legislative process. Supervises the European Commission |
| Council of the European Union (commonly referred to as the Council of Ministers) (see Art. 16 TEU and Arts. 237–243 TFEU) | Makes the final decision on legislative proposals, coordinates economic policies of the Member States, delegates power to other Institutions |
| European Commission (see Art. 17 TEU and Arts. 244–250 TFEU) | Enforcer of the Treaties. Drafts legislative proposals and initiates policy once formulated by the Council |
| European Council (see Art. 15 TEU and Arts. 235 and 236 TFEU) | Now a Treaty Institution because of the Lisbon amendments. A political Institution that represents the Member States and drives reform in the EU |
| European Court of Justice | Hears cases directed to it under the Treaty |
| | Hears appeals on points of law from the Court of First Instance. Rules on matters of interpretation referred to it by courts of Member States |
| Court of First Instance | Hears cases directed to it under the Treaty, including staff cases of the EU |

A key theme when considering the Institutions is the development in the role of the European Parliament, both in legislative power and supervisory power. The European Parliament was previously called the Assembly, and prior to 1979 was constituted of nominated representatives from national parliaments of the Member States.

The introduction of direct elections in 1979 kick-started a process whereby the European Parliament has gradually been given more power and influence in the structure of the EU. This process is motivated by the accusation that there is **democratic deficit** in the EU. Many of the powers are ones that have been added as a result of different Treaties. See the table below for a breakdown of powers and their introduction.

If you encounter a question in an exam that appears to require you to discuss this issue, make sure you are familiar with the relevant development and powers of the European Parliament, and its relationship with the other Institutions (see later in this chapter).

**KEY DEFINITION: Democratic deficit**

The 'democratic deficit' is the accusation levelled at the EU that it lacks democracy in its legislative Institutions. Attempts have been made to address this by reform of the European Parliament. It essentially refers to the fact that prior to 1979, none of the Institutions had directly elected members. The Commission is appointed, the Council of Ministers contains elected representatives (but those elected to national office) and the European Parliament is now the only Institution where members are directly elected by citizens of the EU. This change, and the reforms in the powers of the European Parliament, are intended to address the lack of democratic accountability in the EU.

# Legislative powers

The Commission, Council of Ministers and Parliament all participate in making legislation, a process which also involves other consultative bodies including the Committee of the Regions and the Economic and Social Committee. A summary of the relationship between the Institutions when making legislation is given in Figure 2.2.

A key theme in this area is the way in which the Parliament's role in making law has increased over the past few years. Traditionally the Parliament had very few powers, because prior to 1979 the MEPs were appointed, rather than elected. Successive amendments to the legislative process have increased the involvement of the Parliament so that now, in some matters, the Parliament is placed on an equal footing with the Council of Ministers. Prior to the Treaty of Lisbon, there was a complex list of procedures to be used, which resulted from amendments in successive Treaties. These are listed in the table overleaf.

**Figure 2.2**

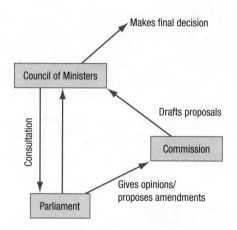

| Legislative procedure | Role of the European Parliament |
| --- | --- |
| Consultation procedure | Parliament has the right to be consulted |
| Cooperation procedure | Parliament has the right to be consulted |
| Introduced by the Single European Act 1986 | Parliament has the right to object to a Council and Commission 'common position' but their objection can be overruled by a unanimous vote in the Council of Ministers |
| Co-decision procedure | Parliament has the right to be consulted |
| Introduced by the Treaty of Maastricht 1992 | Parliament has the right to reject a Council and Commission 'common position' |
| | Parliament has the right to propose amendments |
| | The final decision on the legislative proposal is a 'co-decision' between the Parliament and the Council of Ministers |

**EXAM TIP**

Parliament's involvement in the legislative process has increased with successive Treaty amendments as new legislative procedures have been introduced. If you are ever faced with an exam question which discusses the issue of the increasing involvement of the Parliament in making law, then it is useful to refer to this.

The procedures have now changed, post-Lisbon, as shown in the following table.

| Procedure | Description |
| --- | --- |
| Ordinary legislative procedure (Art. 294 TFEU) | This is what used to be called the co-decision procedure (above) and is now the default legislative procedure. It involves a joint decision being taken between the Council of Ministers and the Parliament, putting them on an equal footing. If there is no agreement, then a Concilliation Committee is used to negotiate a compromise |
| Special legislative procedure (Art. 289 TFEU) | This is either a decision of the Parliament with the Council of Ministers' involvement (in which case a joint decision) or a decision of the Council of Ministers with the European Parliament's involvement (in which case it is the same as the old consultation procedure) |

There is also provision for the Council and Commission to act alone, or the Commission to act alone, in very limited circumstances.

As well as this change in legislative procedures (which has mostly affected the European Parliament's power), as of 2014, the qualified majority voting procedure will be replaced in 2014 by a double majority system.

### Increased role of national parliaments

Article 12 TEU now provides for more direct involvement of the national parliaments in the decision-making process at EU level. They are to be most involved in the area of subsidiarity (the process of making sure that EU law is made at the most appropriate level) but also they are now more formally involved in the process of reviewing draft legislation. Before Lisbon this did happen, but to a limited extent, because of the lack of time given to national parliaments and the sheer volume of legislation.

## Supervisory powers of the European Parliament

The Institutions of the EU exist in a system whereby certain supervision takes place between the Institutions.

In particular, the Parliament, along with increased legislative powers, now also has the power to supervise the European Commission, and has limited supervisory powers over the Council of Ministers.

■ The Parliament has the right to approve the appointment of the President of the Commission and the Commissioners (Art. 17(7) TEU (formerly Art. 214(2) EC), and the right of censure against the Commissioners, enabling them to dismiss the entire Commission under Art. 234 TFEU (formerly Art. 201 EC)

- The Commission is obliged to answer Parliament's questions, and must produce a general report which is discussed by the Parliament (Art. 230 TFEU)

- The Council of Ministers is obliged to report 3 times a year to the Parliament on its recent activity

- The President of the Council of Ministers reports to the Parliament at the beginning of the year

- The European Parliament also runs the Committee on Petitions and appoints a European Ombudsman to investigate maladministration in any of the Institutions of the EU

### REVISION NOTE

The European Parliament, Council of Ministers and European Commission also have the ability to challenge each other's activities through the Arts. 263 and 265 procedure, as they have unlimited standing to bring an action for judicial review under this procedure (see Chapter 4 on judicial review).

The Member States also have unlimited standing under this procedure, and therefore can also scrutinise the Institutions in this way.

# Role of the European Courts

The jurisdiction of the European Courts is split between the European Court of Justice, which has existed since the signing of the European Coal and Steel Community (ECSC) Treaty in 1952, and the General Court (formerly the CFI), which was created by the Single European Act in 1986.

The two courts share the case-load of European cases – the General Court was originally created in order to assist with the growing case law of the ECJ. For example, these courts will deal with matters arising in particular areas (which are dealt with in other parts of this book) such as judicial review under Arts. 263 and 265 (see Chapter 4), enforcement proceedings against Member States (Chapter 3) and will hear preliminary references from national courts under Art. 267 (see Chapter 5). The two courts exist in a hierarchy, as appeals can go from the General Court to the ECJ on a point of law.

### ! Don't be tempted to...

Don't assume that the system of precedent you are used to in the English legal system will also apply in the EU. There is no system of binding precedent in the EU court system, unlike in the UK, where lower courts have to follow the rulings of higher ones. The ECJ, however, does operate a system of persuasive precedent, in that it is unlikely to depart from previous decisions in the interests of consistency but retains the freedom to do so if it feels it is appropriate.

# ■ The relationship between the Institutions

From the above concerning how the Institutions work, we must focus upon the information about how the Institutions relate to each other (Figure 2.3), and therefore how this can have an effect on the operation of the EU. This would also be important in approaching the essay question at the beginning of this chapter. Below are some illustrations of those relationships.

**Figure 2.3**

| Institutions | Relationship |
|---|---|
| Commission and Parliament | Parliament supervises Commission through power of censure and right to ask questions |
| Commission and Council of Ministers | Council submits policy to Commission to be legislated upon and delegates power to Commission through Comitology. Commission drafts legislation |
| Parliament and Council of Ministers | Parliament is consulted on legislative proposals. Council of Ministers reports to Parliament 3 times a year on activity |

 Make your answer stand out

The relationship between the Institutions is rather complex, and certainly more so than can be represented here. However, in order to do well in assessment questions in this area, it is important to examine the subject in more detail. For example, see Lang (2006). This article examines the system of checks and balances referred to as the 'Community method', and argues that part of the criticism of the legal and political safeguards comes from this method being misunderstood. ▶

If you can show that you have an understanding of the relationships between the Institutions, then this demonstrates that your knowledge of the operation of the EU goes beyond the merely factual regarding their composition and procedures.

## Political influences between the Institutions

The Institutions all represent different interests within the EU, and therefore when considering their exercise of powers, it is important to remember who they represent. The European Commission, although appointed by the Member States, is intended to be an independent Institution, free from control of the Member State governments, and representative of the interests of the EU as a whole. The Council of Ministers represents the interests of the Member State governments, and therefore its decision-making will be influenced by them, and the European Parliament is directly elected by the citizens of the EU, and will therefore take into account the interests of citizens. Bearing this in mind will therefore help with understanding the legislative and supervisory processes within the EU.

# ■Chapter summary: putting it all together

## Test yourself

☐ Can you tick all the points from the **revision checklist** at the beginning of this chapter?

☐ Attempt the **sample question** from the beginning of this chapter using the answer guidelines below.

☐ Go to the **companion website** to access more revision support online, including interactive quizzes, sample questions with answer guidelines, 'you be the marker' exercises, flashcards and podcasts you can download.

## Answer guidelines

See the essay question at the start of the chapter.

### Approaching the question

This question asks about the 'Institutional balance' within the EU, and the quote refers to a system of checks and balances operating between these Institutions.

This is intended to allow you to analyse the relationship between the Institutions and the way in which they are able to monitor or supervise each other. You should bear in mind all the discussion about the powers of the Institutions, where they have the ability to monitor each other, and how problems may be dealt with.

## Important points to include

- To answer this question, you need to take into account the following:
- The basic makeup of the Institutions mentioned in the question, and who they represent
- The powers of those Institutions, and how they are able to use them in a supervisory capacity, including:
  - The European Parliament's power of censure over the Commission
  - The requirement for the Council and Commission to report to the Parliament
  - The power of appointment of the Commission of the Council, and the power of approval of those appointments by the Parliament
  - The standing of the Institutions to take action under judicial review against any of the other Institutions
  - An analysis of how this impacts upon the operation of the EU Institutions, especially with regard to how this may influence their decision-making
- You should also take into account the effect that the new office of President of the European Council, along with the new Treaty recognition of the European Council, might have upon your answer to this question – has the balance shifted away from any of the other Institutions?

### ✓ Make your answer stand out

This question will require a certain amount of recall of information about the powers and duties of the Institutions, but in order to make your answer rise above one which merely repeats this information, you need to think about how what you know about the Institutions allows you to analyse the relationship between them. Therefore, you need to think about how the elements of supervision between the Institutions might lead to an overall 'balance' between them.

## READ TO IMPRESS

Dashwood, A. and Johnson, A. (2004) The Institutions of the Enlarged EU under the Regime of the Constitutional Treaty, 41 CMLR 1481

Lang, J.T. (2006) Checks and Balances in the European Union: The Institutional Structure and the 'Community Method', 12 EPL 127–154

Peterson, J. and Bomberg, E. (1999) *Decision-Making in the European Union*. New York: Palgrave Macmillan

## NOTES

# Articles 258–260:

## Enforcement actions against Member States

3

---

## Revision checklist

### Essential points you should know:

- [ ] The purpose of enforcement actions against Member States, and their importance in ensuring the efficient functioning of the Community
- [ ] The substance and procedure of actions to be taken under Articles 258, 259 and 260
- [ ] The exercise of discretion by the Commission regarding Article 258
- [ ] Circumstances where Member States pursue an action under Article 259

# ■ Topic map

# ■Introduction

**An important part of the functioning of the EU is the enforceability of its laws.**

Previously in Chapter 2 we examined the Institutions' involvement in making law and in Chapter 1 we examined the EU's status in the legal systems of its Member States. However, at some point, whether it be deliberate or accidental, Member States run into problems of non-compatibility or conflict with EU law.

In such situations, there are mechanisms involving the European Commission and the Member States, which ensure that the conflict is resolved in the interests of the Single European Market and integration. There is a fairly straightforward procedure for dealing with infringements, and this chapter reviews the procedure for bringing enforcement proceedings and the principles that such an action must abide by, and discusses the reasons behind the procedure and its use. The procedure itself is fairly mechanistic, but the important thing to remember is the thinking behind having such a procedure in place.

## ASSESSMENT ADVICE

**Essay questions** This area is rather descriptive – there is a procedure for enforcing law against the Member States – and it has not tended to be an area which is as appropriate for essay questions as it is for problem questions. However, where there are essays, they may cover areas of the procedure such as, for example, the Commission's exercise of its discretion in using Art. 258, or the effectiveness of the fines system in Art. 260. These types of questions do not merely require you to regurgitate information in the exam, but rather require you to think critically about the procedure and its operation.

**Problem questions** This area of law is one which can be combined with others in such a question, mainly because the problem itself could cover a substantive area of EU law, like free movement of goods or workers, but because of the nature of the problem (if it is caused by a Member State) then Arts. 258–260 may help you to explain how it may be practically resolved. Therefore it would not be unusual for a question to have elements of this area as part of its solution, even though it does not appear to cover this topic.

# ■ Sample question

Could you answer this question? Below is a typical problem question that could arise on this topic. Guidelines on answering the question are included at the end of this chapter, whilst a sample essay question and guidance on tackling it can be found on the companion website.

---

## PROBLEM QUESTION

The German government has recently introduced a system of import licences regarding the import of sausages into Germany. Any sausages with a fat content of more than 20 per cent are refused a licence under their scheme. The German Agriculture Minister, Von Smallhausen, explains to the Council of Ministers that although this is regrettable, it is necessary in order to protect the wellbeing of the German people, and is part of a health policy committed to reducing the cholesterol levels of its citizens.

John Prestwick, the UK Minister of Agriculture, is incensed at this licensing scheme, and believes it is nothing more than a transparent ruse to maintain the market dominance of the German sausage producers and exclude the Great British Sausage from the German market during an economic downturn in meat products.

Prestwick writes a letter to Von Smallhausen, stating that 'unless the German government drops this idiotic licence system, I shall ask the Commission to bring the German government, Parliament and Courts before the Court of Justice for blatantly conspiring to ignore Germany's obligations towards the Free Movement of Goods principle under the EC Treaty. Failing this, the UK government will take this matter before the Court itself'.

When the UK government raises this matter with the Commission, it replies that 'in the light of the current situation with the accession of new Member States into the EU and the effect of the transitional provisions involved in this, it may be better to leave this matter to next year, when the EU as a whole is more settled'.

Advise the UK government as to the possible legal remedies open to it under the EC Treaty.

---

# ■ Purpose of Articles 258–260

The procedure in Arts. 258–260 is there to ensure that where Member States are not complying with EU law, there is an effective system of ensuring that they do comply. This has three elements to it:

- Responsibility and powers as 'watchdog' given to a Community Institution
- Power given to all Member States to take action where they see it is appropriate
- System of fines to back up the system where necessary

The way in which this system is put into practice is through a two-stage process:

- Action taken by, or in front of, the Commission
- Cases taken to the ECJ either by the Commission or by another Member State

**REVISION NOTE**

One other way in which Member States can be liable for their failure to enact EU laws in their own systems is that discussed in Chapter 1: through the doctrine of direct effect. This is different from Arts. 258–260 actions, because it can be pursued by individuals, and Arts. 258–260 cannot. The emphasis is also different as direct effect is about giving effect to the law despite the actions of the Member State, and through the use of state liability for non-implementation, individuals can be compensated for damage which comes directly from the State's failure. Articles 258–260 are about pursuit and punishment of the Member State, rather than compensation for individuals. They are two different ways in which action against Member States can be taken where they are not complying with Community law.

# ■ Article 258 – action by the Commission

**KEY STATUTE**

**Article 258 TFEU**

If the Commission considers that a Member State has failed to fulfil an obligation under this Treaty, it shall deliver a **reasoned opinion** on the matter after giving the State concerned the opportunity to submit its observations.

If the State concerned does not comply with the opinion within the period laid down by the Commission, the latter may bring the matter before the Court of Justice of the European Union.

## Failure to fulfil an obligation

This is not defined in the Treaty. However, you should take a common sense approach to looking at this issue – any duty or obligation placed on a Member State that they have not complied with can fall under this definition – whether that is an obligation directly from the Treaty, or from some form of secondary legislation which has been properly enacted under the Treaty. Also, it can either be an *action* or an *omission* by the Member State. You should also bear in mind that it doesn't matter which part of the State has failed to meet an obligation: the State as a whole is responsible – see Case 77/69 *Commission* v. *Belgium* [1970] ECR 237, where the Belgian government was held to account for the failure of the Belgian Parliament to enact the relevant legislation.

## Member State obligations and the Treaty

All Member States have a general obligation to observe and not contradict Community law. This used to be contained in Art. 10 of the Treaty of Rome, but post-Lisbon this has now been moved to Art. 4(3) of the TEU.

---

**KEY STATUTE**

### Article 4(3)TEU

The Member States shall take any appropriate measure, general or particular, to ensure fulfilment of the obligations arising out of the Treaties or resulting from acts of the Institutions of the Union.

---

This Article is always worth bearing in mind whenever considering any obligation owed by the Member States, not just those under Arts. 258–260, and it binds all organs of the state concerned, including government departments, state-funded agencies, local government, etc.

## Procedure under Article 258

As mentioned above, there are two elements to this after informal discussions have taken place between the Member State and the Commission – action by the Commission, and action in the ECJ. The procedure is shown in Figure 3.1.

| Procedure | What it means |
|---|---|
| Informal letter | The Commission communicates informally and in private with a Member State about a potential breach under the Treaty. The Member State has to cooperate under its obligations in Art. 4(3) TEU |
| Formal notice | Formal written letter from the Commission to the Member State. Sets out what they are accused of, and asks them to respond ▶ |

| Procedure | What it means |
|---|---|
| Member State response | Written response to formal notice. If the Member State fails to respond in 2 months, the Commission goes on to the next stage anyway |
| Commission's reasoned opinion | Formal opinion from the Commission stating what the infringement is, and requiring the Member State to fix the problem. Includes a time limit for them to do so (usually 2 months) |

**Figure 3.1**

## Administrative stage

This procedure must be followed by the Commission, otherwise the Member State has cause to complain about its use of the procedure under Art. 263 or 265. However, if this procedure is properly followed and the Member State does not comply with the Commission's **reasoned opinion**, then the Commission may move on to the next stage of the procedure.

**KEY DEFINITION: Reasoned opinion**

The reasoned opinion is a written statement from the Commission, which lays down the obligation concerned, and the reasons why the Member State has failed to meet this obligation. It should clearly spell out the Commission's objection, and therefore it should be possible for the Member State to know what it needs to do to rectify the problem.

**! Don't be tempted to...**

The important point to make here is the discretion that the Commission has in bringing this procedure. Article 258 says '*If* the Commission considers that a Member State has failed to fulfil an obligation ...' The Commission has a lot of discretion as to when it is going to take action, and for which infringements. Case 247/87 *Star Fruit Company* v. *Commission* [1989] ECR 291 shows that the Commission can't be forced to take action under Art. 258.

There is also no time limit on the different actions of the Commission under the administrative stage, and so it can take the next step in the process when it wishes, if at all. About 90 per cent of all Art. 258 actions are resolved in this stage without going to the ECJ, and the way in which the Commission manages these situations is part of this.

You should bear in mind that as a result an individual cannot force the Commission to take action, but a Member State can take action itself under Art. 259. An individual is better off trying to use direct effect against the Member State, as this allows them to seek a remedy in a national court, and this can be somewhat speedier. Any problems requiring the interpretation of the ECJ can then be referred under the Art. 267 procedure.

When revising this subject, remember that there are alternatives, and that this procedure is part of a wider system. This can be an important point to remember in a problem question such as the one at the beginning of this chapter, but also in an essay question about the Commission's discretion in Art. 258.

**✓ Make your answer stand out**

Commission discretion is an important part of the flexibility of the Art. 258 procedure – the Commission makes its own decisions as to which actions to pursue, but at the same time it means it can go after the more serious infringements first. For further reading on this, see Evans (1979). See also Case 7/71 *Commission* v. *France* for further guidance from AG Roemer on when the Commission might be justified in exercising its discretion not to take action.

## Judicial stage

Once the Commission has exhausted the administrative stage, if the Member State does not comply with its reasoned opinion within the time limit, then the Commission may take the matter to the ECJ. This is the judicial stage.

Points to bear in mind concerning the judicial stage:

- The burden of proof lies with the Commission to prove its case

- Even if the Member State has complied with the reasoned opinion by the time the case comes to court, the Commission may still bring the case: see Case C-240/86 *Commission* v. *Greece* [1988] ECR 1835

- Defences put forward by the Member States are generally not accepted by the ECJ (see for example Case 128/78 *Re: Tachographs* (*Commission* v. *UK*) [1979] ECR 419 – political difficulties involving disputes with the transport unions were not an acceptable reason not to introduce new tachograph laws in the UK). The only acceptable defence is that the Commission got it wrong, and that the State is not in breach of EU law. See also Case 77/69 *Commission* v. *Belgium* and Case C-56/90 *Commission* v. *UK* for other examples.

The outcome of a case in the ECJ is as described in Art. 260, as follows.

**KEY STATUTE**

**Article 260(1) TFEU**

If the Court of Justice finds that a Member State has failed to fulfil an obligation under this Treaty, the State shall be required to take the necessary measures to comply with the judgment of the Court of Justice.

The key thing to remember here is that this therefore provides a clear obligation for the Member State to follow, and removes any ambiguity that the action itself might have uncovered. The Member State *has* to comply – and if they fail to do so, this is where Art. 260(2) comes in (dealt with further on in this chapter).

# ■ Article 259 – action by another Member State

Although the Commission cannot be forced to take action, another Member State has the ability to take the matter to the ECJ itself, if the Commission fails to do so. This takes place under Art. 259.

**KEY STATUTE**

### Article 259(1) TFEU

A Member State which considers that another Member State has failed to fulfil an obligation under this Treaty may bring the matter before the Court of Justice.

## Procedure under Article 259

The procedure (Figure 3.2) followed here is very similar to that of Art. 259. Article 259(2) states that the matter has to be brought before the Commission by the two Member States concerned before it can go to the ECJ, so the Commission still has an involvement here.

**EXAM TIP**

Although the Commission is still involved in Art. 259, remember that it is not able to delay or dictate the timing of the action taken here. This may be important if the Commission refused to take action itself under Art. 258. It is also important to remember this if you are being asked to advise a Member State in a problem question.

**Figure 3.2**

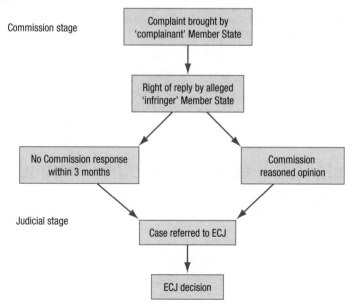

There is a time limit of 3 months, and if within that time the Commission has not issued a reasoned opinion, then the Member State is able to take its case to the ECJ without one.

## Problems with Article 259

There are several reasons why Art. 259 actions can be problematic. Member States are reluctant to take action because of the ensuing diplomatic fallout. It can be a device for forcing the Commission to take the matter further, as shown in Case C-1/00 *Commission* v. *France* where the UK initially said it was going to take action against France for its refusal to lift the beef ban after the BSE crisis. The Commission eventually took action itself.

Article 259 actions that go all the way to the ECJ are rare. This is mainly because it is much more straightforward to get the Commission to pursue the action under Art. 258 (as seen in the *Commission* v. *France* case above). There have only been three cases to date that resulted in a judgment from the ECJ, Case 141/78 *France* v. *UK* [1979] ECR 2923, Case C-388/95 *Belgium* v. *Spain* [2000] ECR I-3123 and Case C-145/04 *Spain* v. *UK* [2006] ECR I-7917.

# ■ Article 260 – enforcement and fines

Usually, a successful action under Art. 258 or 259 will result in the Member State complying with their obligations under the Treaty. In a few very unusual situations it may be necessary to use the enforcement section of Art. 260. This requires two steps to be taken:

- Another reasoned opinion from the Commission has to be issued to the offending Member State
- A second action in the ECJ in order to decide on the fine amount to be imposed upon the Member State

Factors that are taken into account when deciding the amount to fine are:

- The seriousness of the breach and the length of time that has passed since that breach
- The financial size (by gross domestic product) of the Member State
- Whether to impose a lump sum fine, or one which increases daily

 **Make your answer stand out**

Article 260's fines system was only introduced in order to give more teeth to enforcement of Community law against the Member States in more recent times – without it, a State could ignore political pressure from the Community and ▶

continue to act in infringement of their obligations. This system aims to avoid cases lingering for many years. If you are dealing with an essay question on the effectiveness of the enforcement proceedings under Arts. 258–260, then a discussion of the development and effectiveness of the fines system will show a deeper appreciation of the evolution of this procedure. See Wenneras (2006).

# Penalties for failing to implement a Directive – the new regime

Ordinarily the Commission would need to go through two actions in order to impose penalties upon an infringing State (the original Art. 258 action and an Art. 260 action) but now Art. 260(3) has added some teeth to the Art. 258 procedure.

**KEY STATUTE**

### Article 260(3) TFEU

When the Commission brings a case before the Court pursuant to Art. 258 on the grounds that the Member State concerned has failed to fulfil its obligation to notify measures transposing a directive adopted under a legislative procedure, it may, when it deems appropriate, specify the amount of the lump sum or penalty payment to be paid by the Member State concerned which it considers appropriate in the circumstances.

If the Court finds that there is an infringement it may impose a lump sum or penalty payment on the Member State concerned not exceeding the amount specified by the Commission. The payment obligation shall take effect on the date set by the Court in its judgment.

Therefore, if an action is about *failure to implement a directive*, the Commission may apply for a penalty to be levied against the infringing Member State in the first case, and not have to take the procedure around for a second time.

 Make your answer stand out

This new provision is all about tightening up the procedures under Art. 258. Delays in the procedure are an important consideration, and this prevents Member States taking advantage of the fact that lengthy enforcement procedures will allow them more time before they are forced to implement new Directives. If you are faced with a problem question in an assessment involving failure to implement, then this could allow you to show a deeper understanding of how the fines system works, and how it has been updated to deal with States who flagrantly breach EU law.

## Other remedies available in Articles 258–260 actions

Articles 258–260 actions can be very lengthy. Some cases can drag on for years, the most extreme example being the *Commission* v. *France* case [2006] ECR I-2461 which lasted from 1973 to 1994! It may be necessary to make interim orders – those that provide a temporary solution to the problem while the case is still being decided.

| Treaty Article | Description |
| --- | --- |
| Article 278 | Interim injunction from ECJ to suspend a piece of legislation from a Member State that is breaching Community Law |
| Article 279 | Interim measures which can be put in place by the ECJ where there is damage to an individual's interests or economic hardship |

# ■Chapter summary: putting it all together

## Test yourself

☐ Can you tick all the points from the **revision checklist** at the beginning of this chapter?

☐ Attempt the **sample question** from the beginning of this chapter using the answer guidelines below.

☐ Go to the **companion website** to access more revision support online, including interactive quizzes, sample questions with answer guidelines, 'you be the marker' exercises, flashcards and podcasts you can download.

## Answer guidelines

See the essay question at the start of the chapter.

▶

## Approaching the question

This question requires a knowledge of two areas, Arts. 258–260 as covered in this chapter, but also free movement of goods as discussed in Chapter 6. The basic points on free movement of goods will be mentioned here, but you will need to look at the relevant law in that chapter. Remember that this question is asking you to analyse the situation from the point of view of the UK government. Your answer will need to discuss the relevant law with a view to advising the UK government on what they can do as a result of this problem.

## Important points to include

You will need to bear in mind the following issues in your answer:

- The most likely breach of Germany's obligations is through the free movement of goods provisions in Art. 34

- The licensing restrictions are likely to be seen as a measure having an equivalent effect to a quantitative restriction (**MEQR**)

- The claims on protecting the health of the German people are likely to be dismissed following the *Cassis de Dijon* case

- So, you need to look at Art. 258, whether it can be used here, and whether the Commission can be forced to act here – look at the Commission's discretion section (above)

- What procedure would need to be followed? Break it down into administrative and judicial procedure and explain what is needed in each one

- If the Commission is unwilling to follow the Art. 258 procedure, look at Art. 259 as an alternative – what rights do the UK government have to bring the action? Examine the extent to which they can follow this procedure without the influence of the Commission.

- Finally, Art. 260(2) should be used if the German government still refuses to cooperate, as this can impose a fine upon them for non-compliance

 Make your answer stand out

As this is an area heavily dominated by procedure, it is easy just to list the procedure as your answer. However, this will result in an answer that is heavily descriptive and unlikely to impress your examiner. Take some time to think about the policy behind the procedure. The Commission's discretion allows flexibility in the application of Art. 258, for example. Similarly

Art. 259 is used rarely because of the potential for political problems. Examiners like students to have analysed a situation and to be able to produce answers which demonstrate a good understanding of the area, rather than ones that show they have just memorised a lot of facts and reproduced them

## READ TO IMPRESS

Evans, A. (1979) The Enforcement Procedure of Article 169 EEC: Commission Discretion, 4 EL Rev 442 (Art. 169 is the old numbering for Art. 258)

Wenneras, P. (2006) A New Dawn for Commission Enforcement under Articles 226 and 228 EC: General and Persistent (GAP) Infringements, Lump Sums and Penalty Payments, 43 CML Rev 31 (Arts. 226 and 228 are now Arts. 258 and 260)

## NOTES

## NOTES

# Articles 263 & 265:

## Judicial review

4

---

## Revision checklist

### Essential points you should know:

- [ ] The underlying purpose for judicial review actions in the ECJ
- [ ] The Community Acts that can be annulled and the grounds for that annulment
- [ ] The Institutions that can be compelled to act in the absence of action, and the grounds for this
- [ ] The *locus standi* of an applicant for an action under Arts. 263 or 265
- [ ] The unity principle binding Arts. 263 and 265 together

# ■ Topic map

# ∎Introduction

**The ability to challenge a binding Act of the Community through judicial review is an important part of the Community's legal system.**

Articles 263 and 265 contain the main procedures for judicial review of Community law. Although there is no official constitution of the EU, the TEU and the TFEU both confer powers and obligations upon the Community Institutions, and therefore there needs to be a mechanism whereby the exercise (or not) of powers can be reviewed, and the Institutions properly held to account. These procedures have two purposes, either to annul an improperly enacted law, or to compel an institution of the EU to act in a situation where it has not done so, in contravention of its duties under the Treaties.

This procedure is important because of the way that it fits in with the system of checks and balances within the Community – it allows the Institutions, the Member States and individuals to scrutinise Community law and therefore ensure that powers are not being abused.

The purpose of this chapter is to examine these two treaty Articles, the circumstances in which they may come into play, the types of Act which may be challenged, and the grounds upon which they may be challenged. In particular, the rules are more strict for individuals wishing to challenge a **Community Act**, rather than for a Member State or an Institution. This last issue will be dealt with separately.

## ASSESSMENT ADVICE

**Essay questions** Essay questions in this area tend to focus upon some aspect of the judicial review mechanism. This can be, for example, the role this procedure has to play in the checks and balances system set up between the Institutions; it can also be the difficulty which an individual faces in establishing *locus standi* and a discussion of the case law surrounding this issue.

**Problem questions** Problem questions, on the other hand, are more unusual, as they have to involve the creation of a scenario. This therefore can tend to focus upon the *locus standi* issue, as this will involve individuals.

# ◼ Sample question

Could you answer this question? Below is a typical essay question that could arise on this topic. Guidelines on answering the question are included at the end of this chapter, whilst a sample problem question and guidance on tackling it can be found on the companion website.

### ESSAY QUESTION

Community law 'positively discriminates' against any natural or legal person who might wish to pursue an action under Arts. 263 and 265.

Discuss.

# ◼ Article 263: annulment of a Community Act

### KEY STATUTE

#### Article 263(1) TFEU

The Court of Justice shall review the legality of Acts adopted jointly by the European Parliament and the Council, of Acts of the Council, of the Commission and of the European Central Bank, other than recommendations and opinions, and of Acts of the European Parliament intended to produce legal effects *vis-à-vis* third parties. It shall also review the legality of Acts of bodies, offices or agencies of the Union intended to produce legal effects *vis-à-vis* third parties.

Article 263 is the Community's judicial review procedure (Figure 4.1) – allowing the European Court of Justice to review binding Acts of the Community. The purpose of the procedure is to ensure accountability of the Institutions for action taken by them, and to allow different parties to challenge them.

# ◼ Reviewable Acts

Article 263 states that any Act of the Community, other than recommendations and opinions, can be reviewed. With the introduction of the Lisbon Treaty, the law has been changed to accommodate *other Acts of the Community that produce legal effects*. Previously it was restricted only to those Acts found in Art. 288 (formerly 249), however the law has now changed to accommodate the already established reasoning of the ECJ on this matter. The key issue here lies with the binding nature of the Act – recommendations and opinions are not reviewable because they are not

**Figure 4.1**

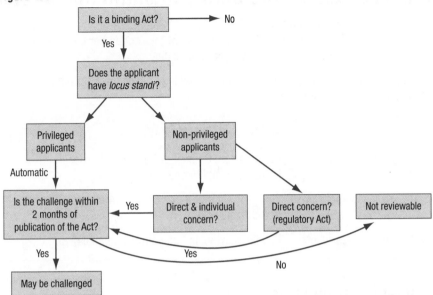

binding. However, any other Act of the Community which produces legal effects can be challenged. For example, all of the following have been held to be subject to review under the then Art. 230 (now 263):

| Name of case | Type of community act |
| --- | --- |
| Case 294/83 *Parti Ecologiste (Les Verts)* v. *European Parliament* | Measures adopted by the European Parliament intended to have legal effects *vis-à-vis* third parties |
| Case 22/70 *Commission* v. *Council* | A resolution adopted by the Council of Ministers to participate in the European Road Transport Agreement |
| Cases 193 and 194/87 *Maurissen and Others* v. *Court of Auditors* | A measure adopted by the Court of Auditors |

**REVISION NOTE**

Only secondary sources of law are dealt with by this area of the Treaty – Treaty Articles themselves cannot be challenged. See Chapter 2 for a fuller examination of those sources of law. In this chapter, where it refers to a 'Community Act', it concerns these secondary sources of law.

# ■ *Locus standi*: the ability to challenge an Act

Probably the most important aspect of Art. 263 (and 265) is the ability to challenge an Act. If you do not have *locus standi*, then you cannot take action here. Lack of *locus standi* will result in a case being thrown out immediately.

For the purposes of Arts. 263 and 265, those eligible to challenge a Community Act are split into three categories:

| Category | Members of this category |
|---|---|
| Privileged applicants | Commission, Council of Ministers, European Parliament, all Member States |
| Semi-privileged applicants | European Central Bank, Court of Auditors, Committee of the Regions |
| Non-privileged applicants | Private individuals (including companies) |

## Privileged applicants

**KEY STATUTE**

### Article 263(2) TFEU

It shall for this purpose have jurisdiction in actions brought by a Member State, the European Parliament, the Council or the Commission on grounds of lack of competence, infringement of an essential procedural requirement, infringement of this Treaty or of any rule of law relating to its application, or misuse of powers.

Those in this category are deemed to have a general interest in Community Acts, and therefore can challenge any reviewable Act. The fact that these parties will all have taken part in some way in passing this legislation in the first place does not disqualify them. This point was made in Case 166/78 *Italy* v. *EC Council* [1979] ECR 2575. The European Parliament has only recently been added to this category, as part of the increase in its influence and power within the Community.

**EXAM TIP**

The exercise of Arts. 263 and 265 is an important part of the system of 'checks and balances' within the Community. In particular, because the European Parliament now has privileged applicant status, it adds to its supervisory powers. Any answer to an essay question concerning the supervisory powers of the

European Parliament (see Chapter 2 on the Institutions) should discuss this issue, and any answer to a question set by your examiners which asks you to comment on the developing powers of the European Parliament should make this point.

# Semi-privileged applicants

**KEY STATUTE**

### Article 263(3) TFEU

The Court of Justice shall have jurisdiction under the same conditions in actions brought by the Court of Auditors, by the European Central Bank and by the Committee of the Regions for the purpose of protecting their prerogatives.

The Court of Auditors and the European Central Bank have always been able to challenge a Community Act if the law in question affects or changes one of their powers. Now the Committee of the Regions is also able to exercise this power.

# Non-privileged applicants

**KEY STATUTE**

### Article 263(4) TFEU

Any natural or legal person may, under the conditions laid down in the first and second paragraphs, institute proceedings against an Act addressed to that person or which is of direct and individual concern to them, and against a regulatory Act which is of direct concern to them and does not entail implementing measures.

Private persons and companies are classed as 'non-privileged' because they have to prove that they should be entitled to challenge a Community Act. This is the most controversial area of this subject, because it very heavily restricts a non-privileged applicant's ability to challenge an Act. The wording of Art. 263(4) has changed slightly from that of the former Art. 230(4). Art. 263(4) allows an individual to challenge an Act where:

■ It concerns an Act addressed to the person

■ It concerns an Act addressed to another person which is of *direct and individual* concern to the applicant; or

■ It concerns a regulatory Act, which is of *direct concern* to the applicant, and which does not entail implementing measures

The previous system under former Art. 230 was very strict, and heavily restricted the type of Community Act which could be challenged. The new post-Lisbon system is broader, but still restricts the circumstances in which an Act can be challenged.

The first of these two categories will be fairly easy to deal with – decisions addressed to individuals are self-evident. A directive or regulation of direct and individual concern must fulfil three criteria: it must be equivalent to a decision, and of direct and individual concern to the person.

## The right to challenge an 'Act'

To see how the new system will liberalise judicial review by individuals, it is necessary to examine the old system. This restricted individuals to challenge only those Acts equivalent to a decision. For example, in Case 41-44/70 *International Fruit Co.* v. *Commission* [1971] ECR 411, it was held that if a Regulation could be regarded as a decision (and therefore was applied like one), then it could be challenged, but ordinarily Regulations have general application, and so cannot be challenged by an individual. Therefore the ECJ would have to be convinced that the Regulation was merely a 'disguised decision'.

The table on p. 65 gives some indication of the European courts' relaxing of attitudes – the case below gives further indication of this.

---

 **Make your answer stand out**

Case C-309/89 *Codorniu* v. *EC Council* [1994] ECR I-1853 relaxed the rules on whether Regulations with general application could be challenged by individuals. Although normally any Act of general application cannot be challenged by individuals, in *Codorniu* the Regulation did have general application, but could still be challenged because it had particular concern to Codorniu. This was a bold move because the ECJ were saying that it had both general and specific applications at the same time. Unfortunately this has not had the effect of generally relaxing the rules, as it hasn't subsequently been followed. The changes to the Treaty in this area do look like they are following some of the principles from *Codorniu* though. A discussion of the development of this area is essential in an essay that asks you to discuss the impact of the *Codorniu* case.

See Arnull (2001).

---

## An Act addressed to that person

Where an Act is addressed to a particular person, then they will have *locus standi* to challenge it. The definition of 'Act' is unclear at this stage, but historically examples of decisions addressed to applicants have been fairly clear. The new concept of 'Act' will broaden this.

## An Act of direct and individual concern to the person

Aside from an Act addressed to that person, if an Act is of direct and individual concern to that applicant, then they can also challenge. Again, the post-Lisbon concept of 'Act' will be broader than previously, but we can use the earlier case law from the old Art. 230 actions to define this concept.

## Individual concern

The definition of individual concern does not come from the Treaties. It can be found in the following case.

---

**KEY CASE**

**Case 25/62 *Plaumann* v. *Commission* [1963] ECR 95**
*Concerning: the test for individual concern*

**Facts**

This was a decision aimed at the German government instructing them to lift an import duty on clementines going into Germany. Plaumann claimed direct and individual concern.

**Legal principle**

They would be individually concerned if the decision affected them 'by reason of certain attributes which are peculiar to them or by reason of circumstances in which they are differentiated from all other persons'.

---

This has therefore been described as defining someone as being part of a 'fixed, closed class'. The main problem that many applicants have had is in defining themselves in this way. There have been various failed attempts by applicants in defining themselves as part of this class. Mostly they have been importers, as in Case 11/82 *Piraiki-Patraiki* v. *Commission*, or Case T-47/95 *Terres Rouges Consultant* v. *EC Commission,* or the *Plaumann* case itself. The argument here was that although these persons defined themselves as importers, anyone could carry out that activity, and therefore they were not part of a fixed, closed class.

## ! Don't be tempted to...

The case law in this area has defined the concept of a fixed, closed class rather strictly. Following on from the test (above) in *Plaumann*, there have been several cases that denied *locus standi* to applicants on this basis. This is an important issue in answering questions on individual concern. For example, following the *Plaumann* criteria, in Case T-47/95 *Terres Rouges Consultant* v. *EC Commission*, the court did not grant standing to a company that had a 70 per cent monopoly in importing bananas – because the class they were in could be joined by anyone else. The key here is: are you in a class that makes you different from everyone else, a class that cannot be joined by anyone else? If so, then you are in a fixed, closed class. Don't fall into the same trap that many of the importers in these cases did, by believing that just because they categorised themselves in a particular way, it would satisfy the test for individual concern. It *must* be a *fixed, closed* class.

If you look at the following case, you can see how an applicant can be shown to be part of a fixed, closed class.

### KEY CASE

**Cases 106 and 107/63 *Alfred Toepfer and Getreide-Import Gesellschaft* v. *Commission* [1965] ECR 405**

*Concerning: the concept of 'fixed, closed class' for an importer*

#### Facts

The applicants had applied for a licence to import grain into Germany on 1 October. The duty on this import was zero, but the German government had asked the Commission for permission to increase the duty. The Commission agreed, and added that in order to do this, all applications made on 1 October would be rejected, and the duty would be imposed from 2 October. The applicants challenged this decision.

#### Legal principle

The ECJ decided that they had standing because they were not just an importer as in the other cases listed above, but because they were part of a fixed closed class – those who had applied for an import licence on 1 October. This went beyond merely being importers as in *Plaumann*, but meant that they were part of a group who were individually affected by the decision.

Aside from the *Codorniu* case above, the European courts have shown a willingness to be more flexible with this concept. Some examples of the application of this are set out in the table below.

| Individual concern | Case |
|---|---|
| As part of a class of political parties affected by the decision | Case 294/83 *'Les Verts'* v. *Parliament* [1986] ECR 1339 |
| If the applicant has been involved in the legislative process used to make the law | Case T-585/93 *Stichtig Greenpeace* v. *Commission* [1995] ECR II–2205 |
| If the applicant is a trade association representing the interests of those who are individually concerned | Case T-447–449/93 *AITEC* v. *Commission* [1995] ECR II-1971 |

## Direct concern

Direct concern merely means that the Community Act is directly applicable to the individual, without any need for the Member States to enact any further laws or have any further discretion. For example, in Cases 10 and 18/68 *Eridana* v. *Commission* [1969] ECR 459, where although this concerned granting of aid by the Commission, the decision as to who was given the aid was made by the Italian government. In this case, the measure was not of direct concern to the applicant as there was a further layer between the measure and the applicant.

**EXAM TIP**

The consequence of such strict requirements for non-privileged applicants is that very few actions may be brought by private individuals. This may seem to be rather harsh, however, when discussing this area, it is worth remembering that there are also important policy reasons for doing this. If the *locus standi* test were broader, then the consequence would likely be the clogging of the European courts with actions brought by those who aren't immediately affected by them. You should bear this in mind, especially if your exam asks you to discuss the position of private parties under this action.

You should also be clear on the potential application of Art. 263 now that it refers to 'Act' rather than 'decision', and is therefore likely to be wider in application than previously.

### A regulatory Act of direct concern which does not entail implementing measures

This is something new to the Treaty post-Lisbon, and therefore the meaning of 'regulatory Act' is not completely clear. It could be that the type of 'decisions in the form of Regulations' that were mentioned in the *International Fruit* case above would fall under this category. The consequence of this is that someone able to show that the Act in question is a regulatory Act which does not require further implementation will only have to show *direct concern* and not *individual concern* as with other 'Acts'.

## Time limit

Article 263(5) sets a time limit of 2 months from date of publication, or from the date the applicant knew about the Act.

## Reasons to challenge a Community Act

| Reason | Example |
|---|---|
| Lack of competence | Each Institution must only act within the powers given to it by the Treaty |
| | See Case C-327/91 *France* v. *Commission* [1994] ECR I-3641 where the Commission signed an international agreement that should have been done by the Council |
| Infringement of an essential procedural requirement | Failing to follow proper procedure |
| | See Case 139/79 *Maizena* v. *Council* [1980] ECR 3393 where the Council failed to consult the European Parliament, where they were obliged to under the Treaty |
| Infringement of the Treaty | A very broad term, which could include all general principles of EU law |
| | Case 101/76 *KSH* v. *Intervention Board* [1977] ECR 797 involved the general principle of the right to be heard |
| Misuse of powers | Where an Institution uses its powers for the wrong purpose |

# ■ Article 265: action for failure to act

Actions under Arts. 263 and 265 are very closely linked under the **unity principle**, therefore the rules concerning how these Articles are used run parallel. They can also be pleaded at the same time, because a failure to act can also be seen as an Institution acting improperly.

## *Locus standi*

The rules concerning *locus standi* are similar but more restrictive than those for Art. 263.

| Article | Applicants |
|---------|-----------|
| Article 265(1) – privileged applicants | Institutions as discussed in Art. 263(2) |
| Article 265(3) – non-privileged applicants | Private individuals as discussed in Art. 263(4) |

**!** Don't be tempted to...

Don't think you can simply analogise Art. 265 with 263. The main problem here is that Art. 265 is even more restrictive than Art. 263, because it doesn't even allow applicants who have 'direct and individual concern' as Art. 263 does. The only individuals who can use Art. 265 are those to whom a decision *should* have been addressed.

**KEY CASE**

**Case 246/81** *Lord Bethel* v. *Commission* **[1982] ECR 2277**
*Concerning:* locus standi *for an individual challenging a failure to act*

### Facts

Lord Bethel challenged the Commission's failure to take action against airline price fixing. The Commission claimed he did not have *locus standi*.

### Legal principle

The ECJ decided that as any decision from the Commission concerning the price fixing would not be addressed to him, then he did not have standing to challenge the Commission's failure to act.

## Reviewable omissions

Article 265 is about duties under the Treaty. So if an Institution has failed to act, and the Treaty states that they should have, then this may be a reviewable omission. It must be a clear duty under the Treaty, and so if this is not the case, then there is no action. For example, in Case 13/83 *European Parliament* v. *Commission* [1985] ECR 1513, the obligation placed on the Commission by the Treaty was not worded precisely enough for a failure to perform this obligation to be a failure to act under the meaning of Art. 265.

## Article 265 procedure

> ! Don't be tempted to...
>
> Where an Institution defines its position, this can be an easy way for it to avoid action under Art. 265. The Treaty doesn't define what this is, but if an Institution justifies why it has not acted, then it may escape the action being brought under Art. 265. The ECJ has held actions inadmissible where this was the case. This is therefore an easy way for an Institution to avoid having to act, and therefore will bring an end to the action. Please bear this in mind when answering an Art. 265 question. The procedure under Art. 265 is illustrated in Figure 4.2.

**Figure 4.2**

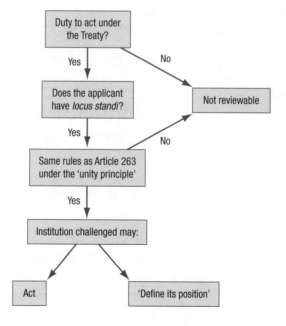

Because the two areas of Arts. 263 and 265 are so closely linked under the *unity principle*, it is worth thinking about when preparing for exams. As long as you are able to identify the few differences between the two actions, then you can consider them together – action taken in the ECJ can tend to include both an Art. 263 and an Art. 265 action at the same time.

# The consequences: Articles 263 and 265

Where an action is successful in either Art. 263 or 265, the consequence is the same: Art. 266 states that the Institution must 'comply with the judgment of the Court of Justice'.

# Chapter summary: putting it all together

## Test yourself

☐ Can you tick all the points from the **revision checklist** at the beginning of this chapter?

☐ Attempt the **sample question** from the beginning of this chapter using the answer guidelines below.

☐ Go to the **companion website** to access more revision support online, including interactive quizzes, sample questions with answer guidelines, 'you be the marker' exercises, flashcards and podcasts you can download.

## Answer guidelines

See the essay question at the start of the chapter.

### Approaching the question

Consider what this question is asking you. As we have discussed in this chapter, the requirements for private persons who wish to take action under Arts. 263 and 265 are much more restrictive than for the Institutions and Member States. You therefore need to carefully consider the restrictions placed on individuals that you will not find placed on other applicants.

## Important points to include

This question is asking you to consider two issues:

- First, the way in which private persons are restricted, through the requirements in the Treaty; that the measure is either addressed to that person, of direct and individual concern to them, or a regulatory Act of direct concern to them. In particular, direct and individual concern has been narrowly interpreted through the use of the phrase 'fixed, closed class'. Look at the key cases such as *Plaumann* and *International Fruit*, and how they have interpreted the meaning of this. Comment on the effect this has had on a private individual's right to bring an action.

- Secondly, consider why the ECJ has been this restrictive in interpreting the Treaty. The *Codorniu* case shows some of the policy arguments behind the way it has interpreted the idea of class. Think about the potential problems of overloading the courts with actions, for example. You also need to consider the other cases listed in this chapter which have shown a more flexible approach to this issue.

- However, you also need to consider the effect the Lisbon Treaty will have had upon the operation of Arts. 263 and 265. Arguably there is a broader approach here because the concept of 'Act' under Art. 263 is wider than that of 'decision' under the old Art. 230.

### ✓ Make your answer stand out

This is an area of law that is heavily based upon the cases. There are many cases which provide good examples of the operation of this rule, for example where they are part of a fixed, closed class (such as Case C-152/88 *Sofrimport*), or where they have taken part in making the legislation (such as Case T-585/93 *Stichtig Greenpeace*), or restrictions on trade associations (such as Case T-447–449/93 *AITEC*). You can make your answer stand out by your use of cases which show the ECJ's development of the law in this area, in particular when considering the post-Lisbon situation, and going beyond merely looking at the most significant cases here. On the issue of Lisbon, also bear in mind that much of the case development is being incorporated into the TFEU in Arts. 263 and 265. Have a look at the wording of the old Art. 230 and 232 and you will see how the Treaty has been subtly redrafted.

## READ TO IMPRESS

Albors-Llorens, A. (2003) The Standing of Private Parties to Challenge Community Measures: Has the European Court Missed the Boat?, 62 CLJ 72

Arnull, A. (2001) Private Applicants and the Action for Annulment since *Codorniu*, 38 CMLR 7

Cooke, J. (1997) *Locus Standi* of Private Parties Under Article 173(4), 6 IJEL 4

Craig, P. (1994) Legality, Standing and Substantive Review in Community Law, 14 OJLS 507

## NOTES

**NOTES**

# Article 267:

## Preliminary rulings in the ECJ

**5**

## Revision checklist

### Essential points you should know:

- [ ] The purpose behind the Art. 267 reference procedure and its use
- [ ] Who may make a reference to the ECJ for interpretation
- [ ] The powers of a national court in making a reference and what must be done with it once received from the ECJ
- [ ] Obligations of a national court in circumstances where a reference is compulsory
- [ ] The ECJ's powers in dealing with a matter referred to them by a national court

# ■ Topic map

# ■Introduction

**Article 267 deals with references made to the European Court of Justice (ECJ) on matters of interpretation of European Community law.**

(Please refer to Chapter 2 for an explanation of the ECJ.) This part of the ECJ's jurisdiction differs from other aspects of its work primarily because Art. 267 references are not cases that the ECJ is dealing with directly, but instead are those dealt with by a national court, which will refer questions to the ECJ.

Article 267 is important because of the consistency of interpretation that it provides. The procedure is a cooperative one, between the ECJ and the national courts of Member States. In this procedure, the ECJ provides the interpretation, and the national court is then given the responsibility to apply that interpretation to the case (Figure 5.1). This ensures that a consistent approach to interpretation of European Community law is maintained, and it creates a clear link between national law and Community law.

**Figure 5.1**

In assessments, you must always be aware of the division of roles in this procedure – each court has an important part to play, and neither court is considered to be in a superior position to the other – there is no hierarchy here, unlike in traditional relationships between courts. Therefore questions can arise which focus upon the relationship between the national court and ECJ in this procedure, or on the respective roles of each court.

## ASSESSMENT ADVICE

When Art. 267 is the sole area examined in question, it will commonly be dealt with as an essay, although it may also form part of a question which touches on other areas as well.

**Essay questions** Both essay and problem questions can focus upon the relationship between the national court and ECJ generally, or concentrate upon one aspect of the procedure. The development of the principles surrounding the issue of what a court of last instance constitutes, or discussion of the *CILFIT* principle (see Case 283/81 *CILFIT and Others* v. *Ministro della Sanità* [1982] ECR 3415) which gives us criteria where a national court may decline the opportunity to make a reference to the ECJ, are both examples which have been used in the past. The *CILFIT* principle and the case it is from are explained later in this chapter.

**Problem questions** Article 267's relevance to wider topics can often appear in problem questions concerning cases before national courts – there can be an argument for making a reference to the ECJ as part of the issues raised by the problem.

## ■ Sample question

Could you answer this question? Below is a typical essay question that could arise on this topic. Guidelines on answering the question are included at the end of this chapter, whilst a sample problem question and guidance on tackling it can be found on the companion website.

## ESSAY QUESTION

The decision of the High Court in *Arsenal Football Club* v. *Reed* [2001] 2 CMLR 23 illustrates very well that the procedure set out in Art. 267 is not an appeals procedure. It was intended to ensure the full collaboration of the municipal courts and the ECJ. This was in order to better develop and enforce EU law in an atmosphere of mutual regard for their relative jurisdictions.

Examine the extent to which this statement correctly states the purpose underlying Art. 267.

# The Article 267 procedure

**KEY STATUTE**

## Article 267 TFEU

The Court of Justice shall have jurisdiction to give preliminary rulings concerning:

- the interpretation of this Treaty;
- the validity and interpretation of Acts of the Institutions, bodies, offices or agencies of the Union.

Where such a question is raised before any court or tribunal of a Member State, that court or tribunal may, if it considers that a decision on the question is necessary to enable it to give judgment, request the Court to give a ruling thereon.

Where any such question is raised in a case pending before a court or tribunal of a Member State against whose decisions there is no judicial remedy under national law, that court or tribunal shall bring the matter before the Court of Justice.

If such a question is raised in a case pending before a court or tribunal of a Member State with regard to a person in custody, the Court of Justice of the European Union shall act with the minimum of delay.

## ! Don't be tempted to...

Article 267 was referred to as Art. 177 previously, and then Art. 234 under the Amsterdam renumbering of the Treaty. Cases will refer to the number that was relevant at the time of the case, and it is therefore important to remember this when reading the judgments of these cases. You will need to refer to the new Article's number, so be careful not to get confused. If you cite an old Article number without any reference to the new numbering, expect to get picked up on it.

The text of Art. 267 is very similar to that of the text of the old Art. 234, although the 'Acts' upon which the ECJ may give a ruling is broader than before. There is one new section which requires speedy action if the matter relates to someone in custody, and it should be fairly obvious as to why the inclusion of this was a good idea.

# ▉ Role of the European Court of Justice

The principle underlying the Art. 267 procedure is cooperation. The ECJ has an important role to play in this, providing a consistent interpretation of matters of European law which is then uniformly applied throughout the EU. The ECJ can answer questions on:

- Interpretation of the EC Treaty
- Validity/interpretation of Acts of the Institutions

It is important to emphasise that the jurisdiction of the ECJ extends no further than the answering of questions put to it by national courts – it cannot proactively deal with matters itself under a strict policy of non-interference. Once it has answered questions put to it, it cannot involve itself with the application of those answers; see *Arsenal Football Club* v. *Reed* [2001] 2 CMLR 23 below.

# ▉ Powers of the European Court of Justice to answer questions

The ECJ has powers to deal with any questions of interpretation that are laid before it by a national court under this procedure. It does not choose the questions, and it cannot influence national courts in their choice of questions. It does, however, have the power to decide that questions are invalid. It can do so on various grounds. Some examples are shown in the table opposite.

As it stands, the ECJ is the only court that hears Art. 267 cases. The Statute of the Court of Justice had previously laid down the possibility for the Court of First Instance (now the General Court) to also hear such cases, and there is a mechanism for review of those cases should any be heard by the General Court.

## The boundary between the power of the ECJ and the power of the national court

The use of Art. 267 is intended to be cooperative in nature, and therefore it is clear that the ECJ interprets, and the national court applies. However, there have been areas where overlap has occurred, causing friction.

| Requirement of a question | Example |
|---|---|
| The question must be necessary for the national court to be able to give judgment | See Case 13/68 *Salgoil SA* v. *Italian Minister of Foreign Trade* [1968] ECR 453 |
| The question must not be a hypothetical one | See Case 244/80 *Foglia* v. *Novello* (No. 2) [1981] ECR 3045, where the ECJ refused a reference on the grounds that the proceedings had created an artificial situation in order to have a question answered |
| The ECJ may select which questions to answer | See Case 6/64 *Costa* v. *ENEL* [1964] ECR 585 |
| The ECJ may not rewrite questions | |
| The referring case must still be active | In order for the ruling to be meaningful, the case must not have been decided before the matter reaches the ECJ – therefore cases are suspended while a reference is made |

### KEY CASE

***Arsenal Football Club* v. *Reed* [2001] 2 CMLR 23**

*Concerning: reference to ECJ; interpretation of EC law; duty of national court to follow ECJ ruling*

#### Facts

The *Arsenal* case concerned a reference made to the ECJ asking several questions on the interpretation of the First Trade Marks Directive 89/104/EC. The case concerned Arsenal suing a seller of unofficial Arsenal merchandise (scarves, replica shirts, etc.) in defence of its registered trade mark in the Arsenal logo that appears on all its merchandise. The referral was made because the UK law on trade marks was based on the Trade Marks Directive.

#### Legal principle

In answering the questions laid down by the High Court, the ECJ also made comments that Laddie J considered to be applying the principles to the facts, which he believed to be outside the powers of the ECJ under Art. 234 (now Art. 267). He therefore applied what he saw as the interpretation, and disregarded anything he considered to be application to the facts. Although his decision was ▶

subsequently overturned by the Court of Appeal, the principle still, in theory, stands – it is not the place of the ECJ to decide the case, but to provide the interpretation to allow the national court to do this.

 Make your answer stand out

Because the *Arsenal* case was overruled by the Court of Appeal, the principle (above) isn't given very much gravity – however, the principle is an important one, and goes to the heart of the Art. 267 procedure. The ECJ must not overstep its role in this procedure to the detriment of the national court's sovereignty.

See Saunders (2004). The significance of this judgment is broader than it at first appears – you can show that you understand the general principle presented by this case, that the ECJ must not overstep the boundaries of what it is entitled to do under this procedure.

There are several different types of Art. 267 procedure (see the following table) which have been introduced in order to speed up the procedure, which is infamous for the length of time it usually takes.

| Procedure | Description |
| --- | --- |
| Simplified procedure | Where the questions referred are identical to previous questions and the answers can be deduced from existing case law |
| Accelerated procedure | Where the national court makes request on grounds of exceptional urgency |
| Urgent preliminary ruling procedure | For questions in the area of freedom, security and justice. Limited written procedure, case mostly dealt with electronically |

## ■ Who may make a reference to the ECJ?

Article 267 refers to 'any **court or tribunal**'. This is not clearly defined, but subsequent cases have provided details as to what this means. Obviously the courts in the main judicial system would fall within this definition, but there are also many other tribunals that may wish to refer issues to the ECJ.

### KEY DEFINITION: Court or tribunal

A court or tribunal should have:

- A judicial function
- Independence from the parties concerned and
- Be recognised by the state for its decision-making function

This is a matter of Community law – it does not matter whether the Member State recognises the body as a court, if the EU recognises it as such. Also look at the *Broekmeulen* case below for further information.

The key elements of what the EU considers to be a court or tribunal are:

- Independence from the parties
- Performance of a judicial function
- Permanence

You should bear in mind that the Member State may not consider a body to be a court or tribunal, but that does not matter, as long as the ECJ considers it to be one.

### KEY CASE

**Case 246/80 *Broekmeulen* v. *Huisarts Registratie Commissie* [1981] ECR 2311**
*Concerning: definition of 'court or tribunal'*

**Facts**

This case concerned the Dutch medical association responsible for registering doctors in the Netherlands. The committee was the appeals committee for the Society, usually regarding the registration of a doctor to practise in the Netherlands. It dealt with cases which had already been through another judicial committee of the Society. Although this was a private body, registration was important because it was not possible to practise medicine in that country without this registration. Broekmeulen had appealed to this committee when his registration to practise was refused. In dealing with his case, a reference to the ECJ was made, and the issue as to whether the appeals committee was a 'court or tribunal' for the purposes of European law.

**Legal principle**

The ECJ decided that the appeals committee was a court or tribunal, despite the fact that Dutch law did not recognise it as such, because, as the ECJ said, it 'operates with the consent of the public authorities and their cooperation, and … after an adversarial procedure, delivers decisions which are recognised as final'. It therefore had all the necessary qualities that the court thought necessary for a body to be considered a court or tribunal for the purposes of EU law.

## Exclusions

There are a couple of specific exclusions – domestic tribunals and arbitrators.

### Domestic tribunals

The element that was missing from Case 138/80 *Re Jules Borker* [1980] ECR 1975, for example, was its recognition by the public authorities. This case concerned a committee of the Paris Bar Association, and in refusing the reference, the ECJ decided that it was 'not handling a lawsuit which it has the statutory function to decide'.

### Arbitrators

Arbitrators are often not recognised as a 'court or tribunal' because parties have usually volunteered to refer their case to arbitration rather than being compelled to do so. For example, Case 102/81 *Nordsee Hochseefischerei GmbH* [1982] ECR 1095 was one where the procedure was **adversarial** in nature, just like the *Broekmeulen* case above. However, because the parties had previously agreed that in the event of a dispute they would go to the arbitrator (rather than the courts), then the ECJ decided that it was not a 'court or tribunal'. This was a private agreement, so the 'public' element was missing, therefore it wasn't a court – the state recognition aspect of the definition was absent.

### EXAM TIP

Although it may seem to be an obvious definition when answering a problem question, it is important to be able to establish definitively that a particular court or tribunal falls within the definition under Art. 267, especially as this differs from national ideas of 'court or tribunal'. Don't assume that the examiner will consider this issue obvious.

# ■ National court discretion to refer

When questions are raised in national courts which concern EU law, the national court has a choice whether to refer to the ECJ. The Treaty puts it as follows:

**KEY STATUTE**

## Article 267(2) TFEU

Where such a question is raised before any court or tribunal of a Member State, that court or tribunal may, if it considers that a decision on the question is necessary to enable it to give judgment, request the Court to give a ruling thereon.

The decision to refer a matter to the ECJ for interpretation lies with the national court. It cannot be compelled to make a reference, either by the parties concerned or the ECJ themselves, in a situation where Art. 267(2) applies.

Any reference made by a national court, however, must be one genuinely needed for the case in hand. For example:

**KEY CASE**

### *Commissioners of Customs & Excise* v. *Samex ApS* [1983] 3 CMLR 194

*Concerning: appropriateness of reference to ECJ; questions to raise*

#### Facts

This case concerned the High Court's attempts to deal with European Regulations concerning an import licence that one of the parties, an acrylic yarn importer, was attempting to secure. In its deliberations, the Court discussed the appropriateness of a reference to the ECJ, and what questions would be in order.

#### Legal principle

Bingham J pointed out in this case that where a party was attempting to use an Art. 267 reference as a delaying tactic, this would justify the Court's refusal to make a reference to the ECJ. This could otherwise be a delaying tactic, based upon the lengthy time it takes a reference to go through the Art. 267 process. The other party would meanwhile be denied a remedy in the matter.

There are several other things to remember for discretionary references:

■ It is unimportant when the reference is made, as long as the case is still active – see Case 35/76 *Simmenthal* v. *Amministrazione delle Finanze dello Stato* [1976] ECR 1871

■ Although the national court does not *have* to make a reference, it will need to clearly explain why, if it is not doing so – see Case 244/80 *Foglia* v. *Novello* [1981] ECR 3045.

# ■ National court compulsory references

There are some circumstances where a national court has to refer questions to the ECJ. As stated in the Treaty:

> **KEY STATUTE**
>
> ### Article 267(3) TFEU
>
> Where any such question is raised in a case pending before a court or tribunal of a Member State against whose decisions there is no judicial remedy under national law, that court or tribunal shall bring the matter before the Court.

In other words:

- If there is no right of appeal and
- There are questions of EU law that need to be answered then
- The national court *must* **make a reference** to the ECJ

> **KEY DEFINITION: Making a reference**
>
> A national court makes a reference to the ECJ by putting together a list of questions for interpretation and submitting them for the ECJ to consider and provide interpretation.

Article 267(3) places an obligation on certain courts to make a reference to the ECJ in certain circumstances. Where a question is raised in a court where it is not possible to appeal, then that question must be referred under the Art. 267 procedure. Such a court is referred to as a '**court of last instance**'.

> **KEY DEFINITION: Court of last instance**
>
> A court of last instance is the last court in a particular court structure to which cases can go. Therefore this means that once the case has been heard by this court, there is no route of appeal to another court. The Supreme Court, as the highest court in England and Wales, is the best example of this in the UK court system.

There have been two approaches to this issue:

| Concrete theory | Abstract theory |
|---|---|
| The court of last instance is one from which there is no appeal in this *case*. | The court of last instance is the only one from which there is no appeal from this *court*. |

## ! Don't be tempted to...

It is important that you clearly understand the difference between *concrete* and *abstract* theory. The abstract theory was initially favoured by the UK judiciary – see Lord Denning's judgment in *Bulmer* v. *Bollinger* [1974] Ch 401, because this meant only the House of Lords fell under an *obligation* to refer questions to the ECJ; however, the ECJ favoured the concrete theory, as shown in Case 6/64 *Costa* v. *ENEL*, whereby if the case at hand cannot be appealed to a higher court then Art. 267(3) applies. Agreement with this approach from judges in the UK can be seen in *Hagen* v. *Fratelli* [1980] 3 CMLR 253 at 255.

### EXAM TIP

The issues surrounding the concrete vs the abstract theories have now been settled, and the UK judges have fallen into line with the thinking of the ECJ, in using the concrete theory (concerning appeal in this *case*). However, as the development of this procedure can be important in any discussion in an essay question, it is still vital for you to understand it, particularly as Art. 267 is still split into mandatory and discretionary references.

# The exception to Article 267(3): the *CILFIT* principle

### KEY CASE

**Case 283/81 *CILFIT and Others* v. *Ministro della Sanità* [1982] ECR 3415**

*Concerning: justification for refusal to make a reference to the ECJ under the Article 267 procedure*

**Facts**

The facts of this case do not aid an understanding of the legal principle.

**Legal principle**

This case considered whether there would be circumstances under which it would not be necessary to make a reference, even where there were questions of European law, and the matter was in a court of last instance. The Court considered that it would not be necessary (under Art. 267(3)) to make a reference where:

- The question of EC law is irrelevant
- The provision has already been interpreted by the ECJ
- The correct application of Community law is so obvious as to leave no room for reasonable doubt

This case shows that it is still down to the national court to make the reference, and still within its power to find grounds on which to refuse to make a reference. The *CILFIT* criteria listed in the above case box are still rather strict though, and therefore they serve to ensure that where the ECJ's opinion does not need to be sought, then the national court does not need to do so.

## ■ The *acte clair* principle

In certain circumstances, the national court may be justified in refusing to make a reference to the ECJ. This is of particular significance if the court would otherwise be considered to be a court of last instance under Art. 267(3). Such a refusal may be justified under the principle of ***acte clair***.

**KEY DEFINITION:** *Acte clair*

*Acte clair* is a term borrowed from French administrative law. This phrase literally means that the law is clear or not in need of interpretation. If something is *acte clair*, then there is no reason to ask for clarification from the ECJ, and no question for the ECJ to answer.

The application of this principle can be seen through the cases. For example:

**KEY CASE**

**Case 28–30/62 *Da Costa en Schaake NV* v. *Nederlandse Belastingadministratie* [1963] ECR 31**

*Concerning: acte clair*

**Facts**

This case concerned a request for a reference to the ECJ of questions which were virtually identical to those that had already been referred in the *Van Gend en Loos* case, and therefore the national court had to decide whether it was appropriate to make a reference in this case too.

### Legal principle

The court decided in this case that if a question is almost identical to one which had already been answered by the ECJ under the Art. 267 procedure, then this will 'deprive the obligation [to refer] of its purpose and thus empty it of its substance'.

### KEY CASE

### *R* v. *Henn & Darby* [1978] 1 WLR 1031

*Concerning: application of* acte clair *principle*

### Facts

This case concerned whether a ban on the import of pornographic materials was a quantitative restriction contrary to Art. 28 of the EC Treaty (now Art. 34 TFEU). The court considered whether reference to the ECJ under Art. 267 was necessary.

### Legal principle

The Court of Appeal decided against making a reference, as previous ECJ case law suggested that this would not be a quantitative restriction under what is now Art. 34. However, when it reached the House of Lords, they did make a reference, and the ECJ decided that it *was* a quantitative restriction. The House of Lords warned about being too keen to decide that something was obvious, and therefore *acte clair*.

### EXAM TIP

There is considerable overlap between the *CILFIT* criteria and the *acte clair* principle in their application, although it is important not to confuse the two. *Acte clair* is more straightforward, as it merely refers to an issue of obviousness, whereas the *CILFIT* criteria are more specific and also include the ability not to refer, even where it's a relevant question, but where it has already been answered before.

# ■ Proceedings after the reference

Once the ECJ has answered the questions put to it under Art. 267, the matter returns to the national court. It is important to consider the following:

- The national court is under an obligation to follow the guidance of the ECJ and apply it to the case at hand (Member States have a general obligation under Art. 4(3) of the TEU to give effect to Community law in general – a broad obligation that covers this)
- The case must therefore still be active until the matter returns from the ECJ
- The national court applies the ruling to the facts. It is not the role of the ECJ to do this instead (see *Arsenal FC* v. *Reed* [2001] 2 CMLR 23).

---

**REVISION NOTE**

Remember: when it comes to applying the interpretation after the ECJ has dealt with the case, it is an issue of EU law that has been discussed. This is where questions on Art. 267 overlap with other areas of *substantive* EU law. The free movement areas, or competition law, are good examples of where this can be the case. You would need to bring in your knowledge of these substantive areas alongside the procedure you have been discussing under Art. 267.

---

# ■Chapter summary: putting it all together

## Test yourself

☐ Can you tick all the points from the **revision checklist** at the beginning of this chapter?

☐ Attempt the **sample question** from the beginning of this chapter using the answer guidelines below.

☐ Go to the **companion website** to access more revision support online, including interactive quizzes, sample questions with answer guidelines, 'you be the marker' exercises, flashcards and podcasts you can download.

---

## Answer guidelines

See the essay question at the start of the chapter.

### Approaching the question

This question asks you to consider the effectiveness of Art. 267 as a cooperative procedure between the national courts and the ECJ, and its effectiveness in dealing with issues of Community law. It is a very open question, but allows you to demonstrate a clear and detailed understanding of this area of EU law. You therefore need to consider examples from cases which may provide you with points about the cooperative nature of Art. 267, as well as bearing in mind the nature of the procedure itself.

## Important points to include

It is important to:

- Be able to show an understanding of the Art. 267 procedure, and the roles of the national court and the ECJ in it

- Discuss any conflicts between the ECJ and the national courts in relevant case law, in particular the problems encountered in the *Arsenal* case

- Discuss the advantages of this system for the interpretation and application of EU law

 Make your answer stand out

This question is one which calls for more than mere reproduction of memorised facts about the Art. 267 procedure, and therefore you need to use what you know about the procedure and issues raised by it to create an analytical discussion of the procedure and its purpose in the EU legal system. Show that your comprehension stretches beyond just what the relevant cases are and what they say – make your answer an integrated discussion of the topic as a whole, and you will show that you really do understand this area, and haven't just memorised a load of 'stuff' to blurt out in your examination answer.

## READ TO IMPRESS

Saunders, O. (2004) A Warning Shot Across the Bows of the ECJ: The Lessons of *Arsenal Football Club* v. *Reed, Legal Executive Journal* 38–40

Tridimas, T. (2003) Knocking on Heaven's Door: Fragmentation, Efficiency and Defiance in the Preliminary Reference Procedure, 40 CMLR 9–50

## NOTES

# Free movement of goods

## Revision checklist

### Essential points you should know:

- [ ] The rules governing free movement of goods in the EU
- [ ] How those rules have evolved in the European Court of Justice
- [ ] The types of measures taken by national governments which will be prohibited by the rules
- [ ] How that applies to individual cases

# ■ Topic map

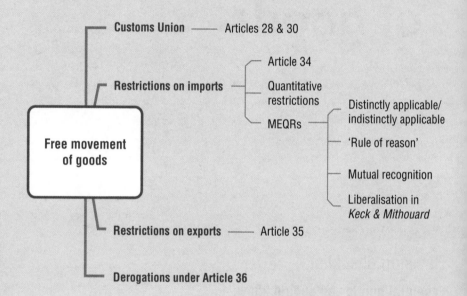

# ▋Introduction

**Free movement of goods is central to the existence of the European Single Market.**

Without this freedom, an important part of the internal EU structure is missing. In order to achieve the free movement of **goods**, the EU has placed restrictions upon individual States' ability to tax or limit the movement of goods across national boundaries. The Treaty prohibits two types of border restrictions:

- Those affecting imports of goods
- Those affecting exports

where goods are being moved from one EU country to another. This is an area covered mainly by just three Treaty Articles, Arts. 34–36, although there is a wealth of case law which has developed as a result of the ECJ's discussion of what is covered by the free movement rules, and what can be justified. This chapter will examine the development of the law from the Treaty through the cases, as often the issues to be discussed in an answer to either an essay-style question or a problem question require an understanding of the rules and how they have developed.

## ASSESSMENT ADVICE

**Essay questions** An essay question on this subject would usually ask you to analyse the concept of free movement of goods through the cases, and therefore would require you to have a good knowledge of the relevant case law in this area. It may ask you to discuss the issues generally, or it may centre in on a particular issue, for example the rule of reason. In any event it will require some form of analysis, and therefore merely reiterating the history of the cases will not suffice.

**Problem questions** A problem question in this area is likely to be one which can overlap with other areas of EU law. For example, one common overlap can be with the Art. 258 action, because if a Member State is in contravention of Art. 34 or 35, this can also be the basis of an enforcement action by the European Commission under Art. 258 (see Chapter 3). Alternatively the question may be one involving a company pursuing an action in the domestic courts, in which case there may also be issues of direct effect (see Chapter 1).

# ■ Sample question

Could you answer this question? Below is a typical essay question that could arise on this topic. Guidelines on answering the question are included at the end of this chapter, whilst a sample problem question and guidance on tackling it can be found on the companion website.

---

## ESSAY QUESTION

Assess the importance the decision in Case 120/78 *Rewe-Zentral AG* v. *Bundesmonopolverwaltung für Branntwein (Cassis de Dijon)* [1979] ECR 649, and by reference to decided case law critically analyse the way in which the 'rule of reason' has subsequently been developed.

---

# ■ Free movement of goods under the EC Treaty

The principle of free movement of goods can be found in Arts. 28–37 of the TFEU. However, this chapter concentrates on Arts. 28, 30 and 34–36, as this is where the main focus of this area lies, both in EU law courses and in assessments.

## KEY STATUTE

### Article 28 TFEU

The Community shall be based upon a customs union which shall cover all trade in goods and which shall involve the prohibition between Member States of customs duties on imports and exports and of all charges having equivalent effect, and the adoption of a common customs tariff in their relations with third countries.

## KEY DEFINITION: Goods

Goods are interpreted as 'products which can be valued in money and which are capable, as such, of forming the subject of commercial transactions' (Case 7/68 *Re Export Tax on Art. Treasures: EC Commission* v. *Italy* [1968] ECR 423 at 428).

Alternatively, goods are considered to be 'manufactured material objects' (Cases 60 and 61/84 *Cinétheque*).

The main provisions concerning free movement of goods are as follows:

| Treaty Article | Function |
| --- | --- |
| Article 30 | Prohibition on customs duties and charges having an equivalent effect |
| Article 34 | Elimination of quantitative restrictions on imports and measures having an equivalent effect (MEQRs) |
| Article 35 | Elimination of quantitative restrictions on exports and measures having an equivalent effect (MEQRs) |
| Article 36 | Derogations from Arts. 34–35 |

## Article 30 – customs union

Article 30 provides a **negative duty** on the Member States not to impose customs duties. Member States need not take any action under this Article, but must not impose any new duties on imports and exports.

---
**KEY DEFINITION: Negative duty**

Many rules of EU law do not impose a duty to do something, but rather a duty NOT to do something – as seen here with Art. 30, this is a negative duty.

---

For example, see *Van Gend en Loos* v. *Nederlandse Administratie der Belastingen*.

---
**KEY CASE**

Case 26/62 *Van Gend en Loos* v. *Nederlandse Administratie der Belastingen* **[1963] ECR 1**

*Concerning: the imposition of an increased customs duty upon goods being imported into the Netherlands*

**Facts**

The goods in question were reclassified by the Dutch government so they became subject to a higher rate of duty. The importers attempted to use Art. 30 (formerly Art. 12, then Art. 25) to challenge the new duty in the national courts.

**Legal principle**

The ECJ ruled that the new duty was in contravention of Art. 30, and that this Article provided a right which could be enforced by individual EU citizens.

---

# Article 34: restrictions on imports

The main area of controversy, however, surrounds Arts. 34–36.

---

**KEY STATUTE**

### Article 34 TFEU

Quantitative restrictions on imports and all measures having equivalent effect shall be prohibited between Member States.

---

**!** Don't be tempted to...

With the renumbering that occurred under the Treaty of Amsterdam, and then subsequently under the Treaty of Lisbon, Art. 30 was renumbered Art. 28 (and is now Art. 34) and Art. 36 was renumbered Art. 30 (and is now Art. 36 again!). This may cause confusion where cases refer to the *old* numbering system – bear this in mind when reading cases decided before the Treaties of Amsterdam and Lisbon came into effect.

Unlike Art. 30, Arts. 34 and 35 required Member States to take positive action to make sure free movement of goods is respected, as well as to refrain from taking action contrary to the principle.

Two types of measure are prohibited by Art. 34:

- Quantitative restrictions on imports/exports
- Measures having an equivalent effect to quantitative restrictions (MEQRs)

## Quantitative restrictions

Quantitative restrictions are easily defined and therefore fairly uncontroversial. A quantitative restriction is one where imports or exports are either partially or totally restricted. This would include quota systems, bans, and also any form of licensing system. Even where the application for an import licence is considered a mere formality, it will still be considered a quantitative restriction because it is a mechanism whereby imports can be restricted. Quantitative restrictions often breach Art. 34 merely because of their effect – they discriminate against imported products, and therefore attract the accusation that they are a barrier to free trade between EU Member States. Because they are very straightforward, they are also rather rare, and have been pretty much eradicated from the EU.

# MEQRs

MEQRs are wider in scope. They add complication to this area because they can be measures which apply to both domestic and imported products. However, it is their *effect* which is important. It is also important to remember that they may not have been intended to have the effect they have by the Member State that has put them in place. Although not defined by the Treaty, there are two definitions of MEQRs:

**KEY CASE**

**Case 8/74 *Procureur du Roi* v. *Dassonville* [1974] ECR 837 at 852**

*Concerning: definition of MEQR*

**Facts**

This case involved a Belgian law which required certain products (such as Scotch Whisky) to be sold only if they had a certificate of origin included with them. The traders involved in this case were prosecuted for selling Scotch Whisky without a certificate, but they had bought it from France, where no certificate was required. The issue was whether this requirement fell within Art. 28 or not.

**Legal principle**

All trading rules enacted by Member States which are capable of hindering, directly or indirectly, actually or potentially, intra-Community trade.

**KEY STATUTE**

**Directive 70/50 Article 2(3)**

Directive 70/50 Art. 2(3) provides a non-exhaustive list of MEQRs, and subdivides them into:

- Distinctly applicable measures (those which apply only to imported goods)
- **Indistinctly applicable measures** (those which apply equally to imported goods and domestically produced goods)

The non-exhaustive list includes:

- Laying down minimum and maximum sale prices
- Fixing import prices at less favourable levels than prices of domestic products
- Exclusion of prices for imports that reflect importation costs
- Requiring an agent to be used in order to access markets in the State being imported to
- Requiring payment or special conditions of imported products which are not required of domestic ones and are more difficult to satisfy ▶

- Requiring imported goods to give guarantees or make payment on account, but not requiring the same of domestic products
- Subjecting only imported goods to conditions that are different from the ones required of domestic goods, e.g. size, weight, shape, etc., and which are more difficult to satisfy
- Hindering purchase by consumers of domestic goods or giving preference to domestic goods
- Precluding importers (either partially or fully) from using national facilities or giving preference to domestic producers
- Prohibition or limitation of publicity for imported products, or preference given to publicity of domestic products

The definition in the *Dassonville* case was very broad, and therefore meant that a lot of actions of the Member States could breach Art. 34, even where they resulted from national differences and were as equally applicable to domestic products as they were to imports. This was a very generous definition which paid no attention to the *intention* of the government in question, but about the *effect* of the measure. The key in *Dassonville* was the potential for the EU to be redivided along national borders by such measures. One major weakness of this definition is a lack of distinction between distinctly and indistinctly applicable measures.

# Distinctly applicable measures

These are measures which apply *only* to imports/exports or goods in transit. It is therefore more straightforward to assess whether they breach Arts. 34 and 35, because in assessing their effect on the market, it is more straightforward to show that their effect is to discriminate in favour of domestic products.

# Indistinctly applicable measures

**KEY DEFINITION: Indistinctly applicable measures**

These are restrictions or other measures which apply equally to imported products and domestic products, for example Case 261/81 *Walter Rau Lebensmittelwerke* v. *De Smedt PVBA* [1982] ECR 3961, where there was a requirement in Belgium for all margarine sold there to be contained in cube-shaped boxes, or the *Cassis de Dijon* case (see below) where all cassis sold in Germany was required to contain at least 25% alcohol.

**KEY CASE**

Case 120/78 *Rewe-Zentral AG* v. *Bundesmonopolverwaltung fur Branntwein (Cassis de Dijon)* [1979] ECR 649

*Concerning: indistinctly applicable measures and their validity under Art. 34.*

**Facts**

A German law prohibited sale of various liquors (including cassis) in Germany with an alcohol content lower than 25%. The claimants in this case attempted to import French cassis into Germany, which had an alcohol content of somewhere between 15% and 20%.

**Legal principle**

The ECJ introduced two principles to address the problems caused by its previous failure in the *Dassonville* case to distinguish between distinctly applicable and indistinctly applicable measures. These would allow exceptions whereby indistinctly applicable measures would not be subject to Art. 28 (now Art. 34) and therefore allow those indistinctly applicable measures to stand. See below for a discussion of the two rules in *Cassis de Dijon*.

# The first *Cassis* rule: the rule of reason

Restrictions would be allowed for *indistinctly* applicable measures if they could satisfy certain mandatory requirements, such as:

- Effectiveness of fiscal supervision
- Protection of public health
- Fairness of consumer transactions
- Defence of the consumer

Examples of this approach were discussed in the following cases:

| Case | Exception under the rule of reason |
|---|---|
| Cases 60 and 61/84 *Cinétheque SA* v. *Fédération Nationale des Cinémas Françaises* [1985] ECR 2605 | Protection of a Member State's culture |
| Case 302/86 *EC Commission* v. *Denmark* [1988] ECR 4607 | Protection of the environment |

▶

| Case | Exception under the rule of reason |
|------|-----------------------------------|
| Case C-169/91 *Stoke-on-Trent City Council and Another* v. *B&Q Plc* [1993] 1 CMLR 426 | Socio-cultural characteristics of a country |
| Case 120/78 *Rewe-Zentral AG* v. *Bundesmonopolverwaltung für Branntwein (Cassis de Dijon)* [1979] ECR 649 | Protection of public health |

The general rule appears to be that if a measure is necessary, then it can be allowed under the rule of reason. Necessary = proportionate so, for example, the ban in *Cassis* was not proportionate, as labelling would have been enough to protect the health of consumers, but the restriction in *Cinétheque* was proportionate.

**EXAM TIP**

Because the rule of reason does not provide an exhaustive list of examples of measures which would be allowed, the rule itself and the cases that followed it can only give examples of what has been permitted in the past. Therefore if you are faced with a problem question on this subject, the scenario could also be one which falls under the rule – but it is up to you to argue the case that it is proportionate if there is no similar case to cite in example.

## The second *Cassis* rule: mutual recognition

Under the second rule in *Cassis*, provided the products have been lawfully introduced into one Member State, then there should be no reason why they should not be imported into another. For example:

| Case | Example |
|------|---------|
| Case 16/83 *Criminal Proceedings Against Prantl* [1984] ECR 1299 | Import of Italian wine into Germany in bottles whose shape was normally restricted. This was allowed because the wine was legally marketed in Italy |
| Case 261/81 *Walter Rau Lebensmittelwerke* v. *De Smedt PVBA* [1982] ECR 3961 | Belgian law restricting margarine to cube-shaped tubs prohibited because margarine was lawfully sold in other types of packaging elsewhere in the EU |
| Case 178/84 *Commission* v. *Germany (Beer Purity Laws)* [1987] ECR 1227 | Beer from other EU states that did not comply with the German beer purity law could be imported and could be called beer because it was lawfully sold in other EU States |

**Make your answer stand out**

The decision in *Cassis de Dijon* highlighted an important issue concerning Art. 34 – that the judgment in *Dassonville* was far too broad in its scope, and therefore there were some indistinctly applicable measures which should be excused despite being breaches of Art. 34 under the *Dassonville* formula. You can therefore use this point to show how the law has developed from the very simplistic position presented by the *Dassonville* formula to a more sophisticated understanding of how free movement of goods laws should be applied in the Union.

See Gormley (1981) and Weiler (1999).

# The liberalisation of Article 34 and indistinctly applicable measures

**KEY CASE**

**Cases C-267 and C-268/91 *Keck & Mithouard* [1993] ECR 1-6097**

*Concerning: indistinctly applicable measures under Art. 34 (at that time Art. 28)*

**Facts**

A French law prohibited the resale of goods that had not been altered or repackaged at a price lower than the price at which they had been bought, in order to prevent so-called 'predatory pricing' (the process of making a short-term loss in order to force competition out of the market).

The measure was challenged as being contrary to Art. 34, and the ECJ modified its approach to indistinctly applicable measures on the grounds that traders had increasingly used these laws to challenge limits to their commercial freedom.

**Legal principle**

Where a measure was indistinctly applicable, if that measure constituted a 'selling arrangement', then it would not breach Art. 34.

The phrase 'selling arrangement' has not been clearly defined. There are, however, cases which have distinguished between selling arrangements and other product-related requirements, with the latter falling outside the principle in *Keck*.

| Selling arrangements | Other product related requirements to be met |
|---|---|
| Case C-292/92 *Hünermund*: prohibition on pharmacies advertising certain pharmaceutical products outside their premises<br><br>Case C-412/93 *Leclerc-Siplec*: prohibition on television advertising for certain products | Case C-470/93 *Vereingegen Unwesen in Handel* v. *Mars*: prohibition on certain advertising claims on packaging.<br><br>Case C-366/04 *Schwarz*: requirement to individually package chewing gum dispensed by a vending machine |

 Make your answer stand out

The *Keck* case at first glance appears to be doing nothing more than splitting indistinctly applicable measures into two further sub-groups; however, the case was significant in that it halted the advanced use of Art. 34 by traders where they were challenging national rules only because they limited their commercial freedom. For example, see the Sunday trading cases where DIY retailers were using European law to directly challenge the Sunday trading rules in the UK:

- Case C-145/88 *Torfaen Borough Council* v. *B&Q Plc* [1989] ECR 3851
- Case C-169/91 *Stoke-on-Trent City Council* v. *B&Q Plc* [1992] ECR I-6635
- *Wellingborough Borough Council* v. *Payless DIY Ltd* [1990] 1 CMLR 773

*Keck* was therefore further refining the rules concerning national differences and creating a situation whereby such differences were not to be removed just because the rules in one country were stricter than in others. This then ties in with the need for a proportionate approach – remember that the free movement of goods principles are not there to eradicate national difference just for the sake of it, and because of the *Keck* judgment, it is clear that the law now makes allowances where those differences are justified. So if you are faced with this issue in a problem question, you can ensure that you are applying the law correctly, and going beyond the *Dassonville* judgment. If you are dealing with an essay, then the finer application of free movement law presented by *Keck* can allow you to demonstrate your understanding of the evolution of EU law.

See Chalmers (1994) and Gormley (1994).

**EXAM TIP**

The three cases of *Dassonville, Cassis de Dijon* and *Keck & Mithouard* form the basis of the development of the law in the area of Art. 34. It is therefore essential that these cases form part of your revision on this topic – not only will they help you to understand how this area has evolved, but it will also demonstrate to the examiner that you have an understanding of how Art. 34 has been applied to the cases. The rest of the case law should also form part of your revision, but you will find it more straightforward if you use these three cases as your starting point.

# Article 35: restrictions on exports

**KEY STATUTE**

**Article 35 TFEU**

Quantitative restrictions on exports, and all measures having equivalent effect, shall be prohibited between Member States.

Unlike Art. 34 (see Figure 6.1), there are no indistinctly applicable measures, and the *Dassonville* test does not apply. A measure has to have as its specific object the restriction of intra-Community trade (that is, trade between Member States), and therefore it is a lot more difficult to argue this than with Art. 34. Only measures which can be shown to be protectionist will breach Art. 35.

# Article 36: derogations from Articles 34 and 35

**KEY STATUTE**

**Article 36 TFEU**

The provisions of Arts. 34 and 35 shall not preclude prohibitions or restrictions on imports, exports or goods in transit justified on grounds of public morality, public policy or public security; the protection of health and life of humans, animals or plants; the protection of national treasures possessing artistic, historical or archaeological value; or the protection of industrial and commercial property. Such prohibitions or restrictions shall not, however, constitute a means of arbitrary discrimination or a disguised restriction on trade between Member States.

Article 36 provides situations where Member States may be excused something which is a restriction of Art. 34 or 35. However:

■ The list in Art. 36 is *exhaustive*

■ Proven ulterior motives can prevent a restriction being justified under Art. 36

**Figure 6.1**

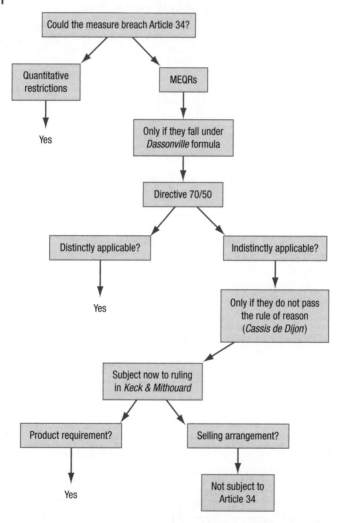

■ Where rules have been harmonised at Community level, then a measure may not be justified under Art. 36

■ Provisions are narrowly construed and must satisfy the test of proportionality

Examples of each of the areas on the list are as follows:

| Article 36 justification | Case |
|---|---|
| Public morality | Compare *R* v. *Henn & Darby* (justified prohibition on pornography due to illegality in the UK) with:<br><br>*Conegate* v. *Customs & Excise* (prohibition not justified as products were not prohibited in UK) |
| Public policy | *R* v. *Thompson* (restriction on export of collector's coins justified because of the need to protect mint coinage) |
| Public security | Case 72/83 *Campus Oil Ltd* (requirement for importers of petroleum to buy 35% of their products from the nationalised refinery allowed Ireland to maintain the ability to refine petroleum, an important security consideration) |
| Protection of life or health of humans, animals and plants | Case 4/75 *Rewe-Zentralfinanz GmbH* v. *Landwirtschaftskammer* [1975] ECR 843 (inspection requirement which only applied to imported apples was justified because of the real risk to health from something which was not present in domestic apples) |
| Protection of national treasures possessing artistic, historical or archaeological value | Case 7/68 *Re Export Tax on Art Treasures* [1968] ECR 423 (quantitative restriction on export of art treasures was justified, but a tax was not) |
| Protection of industrial and commercial property | Case 78/70 *Deutsche Grammophon Gesellschaft mbH* v. *Metro-SB-Grossmarkte GmbH* [1971] ECR 487 |

# ■Chapter summary: putting it all together

## Test yourself

☐ Can you tick all the points from the **revision checklist** at the beginning of this chapter?

☐ Attempt the **sample question** from the beginning of this chapter using the answer guidelines below.

☐ Go to the **companion website** to access more revision support online, including interactive quizzes, sample questions with answer guidelines, 'you be the marker' exercises, flashcards and podcasts you can download.

# Answer guidelines

See the essay question at the start of the chapter. A diagram illustrating how to structure your answer is available on the companion website.

## Approaching the question

This question asks you specifically to examine the *Cassis de Dijon* case, but within the context of the law on free movement of goods, and including a discussion of how the law has developed since then. Just because the *Cassis* case is the one mentioned does not mean that this is the only case law that needs to be discussed – this question would allow you to demonstrate your understanding of the area as a whole, through a discussion of this case's place in it. You should therefore be prepared to analyse cases both before and after this judgment. Think about how you can discuss this case and its place in the development of EU law in this area.

## Important points to include

An approach to this question could include the following points:

- An introduction summarising the area of law and pointing out the important issues to be discussed in your answer; in this case, it will be centred on Art. 34

- A discussion of the issues raised by the inclusion of indistinctly applicable and distinctly applicable measures under Art. 34

- An assessment of the importance of the *Cassis* case, including a discussion of:

  - The decision made in the case itself

  - The issues raised by that decision which are of more general application

- An evaluation of how that decision may have changed the law in the area, and the significance of that change

- The cases which have followed on from *Cassis*, and how they may have changed the application of *Cassis* in EU law today

- A conclusion which summarises the issues and the relevance of the *Keck* decision to current application of EU law

**Make your answer stand out**

Where you are asked to answer an essay question where a specific case is mentioned in the title, there is often the temptation to write everything and anything you know about that case without thought as to structure or as to how that is going to answer the question. It is important that an answer to a question of this type has a clear logic, and that you see through the case to the context in which it sits, and are able to use the case to critically evaluate the area of law in question. Being able to produce a meaningful discussion using the case and related cases will make your answer stand out.

## READ TO IMPRESS

Chalmers, D. (1994) Repackaging the Internal Market – the Ramifications of the *Keck* Judgement, 19 EL Rev 385

Gormley, L.W. (1981) *Cassis de Dijon* and the Communication from the Commission, 6 EL Rev 454

Gormley, L.W. (1994) Reasoning Renounced? The Remarkable Judgment in *Keck and Mithouard*, EBLR 63

Steiner, J. (1992) Drawing the Line: Uses and Abuses of Article 30 EEC, 29 CML Rev 749

Weatherill, S. (1996) After *Keck*: Some Thoughts on How to Clarify the Clarification, 33 CML Rev 885

Weiler, J.J. (1999) From *Dassonville* to *Keck* and Beyond: An Evolutionary Reflection on the Text and Context of the Free Movement of Goods, in P. Craig and G. de Burca (eds) *The Evolution of EU Law*, Oxford University Press, Oxford, Chapter 10

## NOTES

# Free movement of workers

7

## Revision checklist

**Essential points you should know:**

☐ The basis and purpose of free movement of workers and their families within the EU

☐ The rules concerning the right of an EU citizen to move freely within the EU for work

☐ Any restrictions upon that freedom of movement and their purpose

☐ Rules covering the freedom of movement of family or dependants of a worker

# ■ Topic map

# ■ Introduction

**Free movement of workers is one of the fundamental freedoms of the Single European Market.**

It was originally established to complement the other freedoms (goods, capital, services) and therefore promote economic activity within the Community, but can also be seen as an important right for individuals who are EU citizens, to allow them and their families to move freely throughout the Community without restrictions. Through Directive 2004/38, the concept is gradually being transformed into a more general one of citizenship, which works through consideration of other freedoms alongside this one. However, economic activity of persons moving around the EU remains one of the most important aspects here. This chapter reviews the rules concerning freedom of movement of persons classed specifically as **workers**, although a broader concept of free movement of persons can be seen if you consider free movement of services too. Some of the secondary legislation does not distinguish between employed persons and self-employed persons (who are dealt with through the rules concerning 'establishment'). We will also be examining the situations in which a person may bring their family or dependants along when migrating between Member States, and any restrictions that the Member States are allowed to impose upon individuals attempting to move between Member States for work.

Where this area is assessed, it can appear in exam questions as a discrete subject of itself, but as with most EU law, can also overlap into other areas. It is not a complex area of EU law, and you can get a good grasp of the principles through an appreciation of how the law applies to everyday life in the EU.

## ASSESSMENT ADVICE

Questions in this area generally take the form of scenario-based **problem questions**. A question will usually involve a situation covering a person and their family either working or attempting to work in a Member State other than their own, and the application of the rules to their situation. It is most important to be familiar with the concept of 'worker' under the Treaty and relevant secondary legislation, along with the derogations and how they may be applied to the worker. The status of family members may also be raised as an issue in a problem question, so it is important to know the rules concerning which family members are also entitled to residence as dependants of the worker.

# ■ Sample question

Could you answer this question? Below is a typical problem question that could arise on this topic. Guidelines on answering the question are included at the end of this chapter, whilst a sample essay question and guidance on tackling it can be found on the companion website.

---

### PROBLEM QUESTION

Stefan, a Danish national, and Juanita, a Portuguese national, have been living together for three years in Denmark. They decide to try and work in the UK, and move to Manchester for this purpose.

After trying to find work for three months without success, Juanita gives up and decides to enrol at the local college in order to study fashion design. Her application for financial assistance is refused as she is not a national of the country. She invites her Brazilian grandmother, Tatiana, to stay with them in Manchester, but on her arrival in the UK, Tatiana is refused entry.

Stefan, in the meantime, has found part-time work as a parcel courier, but Juanita is asked to leave the country, as she and Stefan are not married. Further, Stefan's employer is suspected of using his business to cover a drug smuggling ring, and as a result, Stefan is rounded up by the police and recommended for deportation as 'undesirable'.

Advise Stefan, Juanita and Tatiana of their rights in EU law.

---

# ■ Free movement of workers under the EC Treaty

The concept of free movement of workers is enshrined in the Treaty as one of the four fundamental freedoms. The freedom itself is contained in Art. 45 of the Treaty, along with the powers given to the EU to make secondary legislation on the matter in Art. 46.

---

### KEY STATUTE

**Article 45(1) and (2) TFEU**

(1) Freedom of movement for workers shall be secured within the Community.
(2) Such freedom of movement shall entail the abolition of any discrimination based on nationality between workers of the Member States as regards employment, remuneration and other conditions of work and employment.

---

This Article makes three important points:

- A worker is entitled to move freely throughout the Community for the purposes of getting a job and performing that job (Art. 45(1) and (3))
- A worker has the right not to be discriminated against based on their nationality (Art. 45(2))
- That right is subject to several exceptions (Art. 45(2) and (4))

This Article, however, does not contain a lot of detail concerning how this is to be put into practice (it does not even define 'worker', for example) and therefore there is a right contained in Art. 46 giving the EU the right to make secondary legislation in order to provide the detail needed.

# ■ Free movement of workers under secondary legislation

Free movement of workers is primarily dealt with through the secondary legislation, Regulation 1612/68, and Directive 2004/38. The role of these pieces of legislation is to provide the detail that the EC Treaty does not provide.

# ■ Definition of 'worker'

When dealing with this area, the first thing you must establish is that the person concerned is classed as a **worker**. In most circumstances, this will be a fairly straightforward question, although in some cases the answer is not as obvious as appears. If we start from basic principles, a worker can be defined as follows:

**KEY DEFINITION: Worker**

Workers are EU nationals who are either in employment (full or part time) in that they are paid in return for their performance under an employer/employee relationship, or are seeking actual paid work.

This definition does not come from the Treaty, but can be explained by the case law surrounding this area. Article 45 failed to define what a worker was, and therefore the ECJ has taken a broad approach to defining 'worker' through the case law. Below are some examples of decisions from the ECJ on the definition of 'worker', but first, the *Lawrie-Blum* case provides a general explanation.

**KEY CASE**

**Case 66/85 *Lawrie-Blum* v. *Land Baden-Württemburg* [1986] ECR 2121**

*Concerning: definition of 'worker' under Article 45*

**Facts**

This case concerned a trainee teacher in Germany. The German government attempted to argue that Lawrie-Blum was not a 'worker' because of his trainee status.

**Legal principle**

The ECJ found that the trainee teacher was a 'worker,' and set out a three-part test to deal with the issue. They defined a 'worker' as someone who:

(1) during a certain period of time
(2) performs services for and under the direction of another
(3) in return for remuneration.

Other case law has also taken this broad approach to defining a worker. The concept of worker has two parts, an economic part and a formal part

# Economic aspect of 'worker'

A worker has to be performing duties in exchange for some economic gain, whether that be money or otherwise. The table gives examples of how the courts have dealt with the economic part of this.

| Case | Principle |
| --- | --- |
| Case 53/81 *Levin* v. *Staatssecretaris van Justitie* [1982] ECR 1035 | The definition of worker included those doing part-time work |
| Case 196/87 *Steymann* v. *Staatssecretaris van Justitie* [1988] ECR 6159 | Payment for work did not have to be monetary, but could be a benefit in kind |
| Case 139/85 *Kempf* v. *Staatssecretaris van Justitie* [1986] ECR 1741 | Someone who does not earn enough to live on (and therefore must also claim benefits) is still a worker |

# Formal aspect of 'worker'

On the formal aspect, a worker must be someone defined as 'employed'. Therefore, you would expect an employer/employee relationship to exist, with the employee taking instructions from the employer.

| Case | Principle |
|------|-----------|
| Case 66/85 *Lawrie-Blum* v. *Land Baden-Württemburg* [1986] ECR 2121 | Someone who performs a service under the direction of another |
| Case 75/63 *Hoekstra* v. *BBDA* [1964] ECR 177 | A worker could also be someone who had recently lost their job, and was looking to take another one |

# Working and seeking work

It is often necessary to enter a Member State in order to get work, so those looking for work are treated in a similar fashion to workers, but only for a limited time.

> **KEY CASE**
>
> **Case C-292/89 *R* v. *Immigration Appeal Tribunal ex parte Antonissen* [1991] ECR I-745**
>
> *Concerning: status as 'worker' when seeking work in another Member State*
>
> **Facts**
>
> Antonissen was appealing against a decision to deport him, claiming free movement as a worker under Art. 48 (then 39, now Art. 45) as he had been looking for work in the UK. However, he had not found any for over 6 months.
>
> **Legal principle**
>
> The ECJ held that it was reasonable for the Member State to deport someone if they had not found work within 6 months.

Article 6 of Directive 2004/38 allows any EU national to remain in any Member State for up to 3 months without having to conform to the definition of 'worker', but beyond this, unless there is a realistic chance of them getting a job, they can be required to leave the State concerned.

**EXAM TIP**

The simple answer to the issue of seeking work is to apply a time limit of 3 months, because from Directive 2004/38 it appears reasonable to come to this conclusion. However, this is a grey area, because if a person can show that they are *seeking* employment, and have a realistic chance of getting a job, then they may be able to show they have a right to stay, even though the 3 months has expired. Deeper thinking like this will enable you to show a better understanding of the subject when tackling an exam question. The point about the time limit was emphasised in Case C-138/02 *Brian Francis Collins* v. *Secretary of State for Work and Pensions* [2004] ECR I-2703, so in theory a person could stay in a Member State a lot longer, although the Member State is allowed to lay down a reasonable time limit.

# ■ Rights of a worker

**KEY STATUTE**

**Article 45(3) TFEU**

3 It shall entail the right, subject to limitations justified on grounds of public policy, public security or public health:
   (a) to accept offers of employment actually made;
   (b) to move freely within the territory of Member States for this purpose;
   (c) to stay in a Member State for the purpose of employment in accordance with the provisions governing the employment of nationals of that State laid down by law, regulation or administrative action;
   (d) to remain in the territory of a Member State after having been employed in that State, subject to conditions which shall be embodied in implementing regulations to be drawn up by the Commission.

The rights outlined above are dealt with generally by Directive 2004/38. All rights concerning movement into or out of a Member State are subject to the need to have a valid passport. In summary, the most important of these rights are:

| Right | Source |
|---|---|
| Right to enter | Article 5(1) Directive 2004/38 |
| Right to leave | Article 4(1) Directive 2004/38 |
| Right to reside | ■ Without a job (up to 3 months): Article 6 Directive 2004/38<br><br>■ With a job: Article 7 Directive 2004/38 |
| Right to remain after losing a job | Article 7(3) Directive 2004/38, if:<br><br>■ Temporarily unable to work because of illness<br><br>■ Involuntarily unemployed and seeking work<br><br>■ Started vocational training |
| Right of permanent residence | Article 16(1) Directive 2004/38 after continuous residence of 5 years |

## Public sector work

Jobs in the public sector are specifically excluded under Art. 45(4). It is important for the government of a country to restrict certain public sector jobs to their own nationals.

## Non-discrimination under Article 45(2)

**KEY STATUTE**

**Article 45(2) TFEU**

Such freedom of movement shall entail the abolition of any discrimination based on nationality between workers of the Member States as regards employment, remuneration and other conditions of work and employment.

Regulation 1612/68 outlaws many obstacles to migrant workers in its first 12 Articles. This therefore means that a worker is allowed access to the same jobs, tax and social advantages as if they were a national of that country. However, Member States are justified in withholding social assistance (including financial) during the first 3 months of the worker's residence (see Art. 24(2) of Directive 2004/38). They can also withhold any financial support for training or studying until the worker has permanent residence rights.

# ■ Rights of family members and dependants

When a worker moves within the Single Market, of course their family and dependants will need to move as well. The Treaty does not mention family members. However, Art. 2(2) Directive 2004/38 gives details of family members and dependants who have the right to move into the Member State with the worker (Figure 7.1).

## ! Don't be tempted to...

When considering descendants and dependants under 21, it is important to note that children of either the worker or their spouse have particularly special status: the term 'children' includes all children of either partner, not just those who are common to both the worker and their partner. They also remain part of the worker's family, even after a divorce has taken place. They are also protected by Art. 8 of the European Convention on Human Rights, which protects the right to family life. Article 12 Directive 2004/38 also gives them the same right to education as nationals of that State. Consider carefully the rights of these dependants, and make sure you are aware of how the rules apply to them.

## ✓ Make your answer stand out

The situation concerning family members can become complicated – because their status will be dependent upon the status of the worker, and in this way they can be disadvantaged. You must therefore think carefully about their status, and deal with the status of the worker first before dealing with the dependant. This will prevent you contradicting yourself in your answer, particularly if that issue is in the exam. See Woods (1999).

**Figure 7.1**

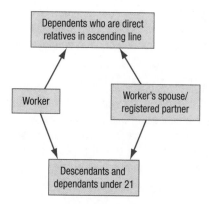

# ■ Derogations from free movement of workers

**KEY DEFINITION: Derogation**

The exemption from, or the relaxation of, a particular law. In this context, exceptions to the rule requiring free movement for workers.

The right of free movement for workers is not absolute – you also have to bear in mind that there are some circumstances in which a Member State can either refuse entry to a worker, or require them to leave. If you look at Art. 45(3), it refers to the rights of a worker being generally 'subject to limitations justified on grounds of public policy, public security or public health'. This is quite a vague phrase, and Directive 2004/38 deals with specifics of how it is to be applied. It is possible to see its influence in refining these quite general concepts.

## Public policy and public security

The public policy ground for excluding migrant workers is probably the vaguest of the three **derogations**, and therefore potentially most open to abuse by a Member State that wants to justify excluding someone. Public security is also generally considered at the same time, as the two concepts overlap. The ECJ's approach has been to give the public policy ground for exclusion a very narrow meaning. Have a look at the evolution of this concept in the table below.

| Case/Article | Meaning of 'public policy' |
| --- | --- |
| Case 41/74 *van Duyn* v. *Home Office* [1974] ECR 1337 | Activities/membership of an organisation considered to be 'socially harmful' |
| Case 30/77 *R* v. *Bouchereau* [1977] ECR 1999 | Activities which are a genuine and sufficiently serious threat to the requirements of public policy affecting one of the fundamental interests of society |
| Article 27(2) Directive 2004/38 | 'Must represent a genuine, present and sufficiently serious threat affecting one of the fundamental interests of society' |

There are also several other considerations under Directive 2004/38. Member States are not allowed to use the public policy derogation in the following circumstances:

| Article of Directive 2004/38 | Exception |
| --- | --- |
| Article 15(2) | Not having a passport or ID card is not grounds for expelling a person |
| Article 27(1) | Prohibits excluding a person for economic purposes |
| Article 27(2) | Previous criminal convictions on their own are not enough to exclude a person |

## Conduct of the person

A reason for excluding someone under public policy or public security has to be based on the conduct or behaviour of the person concerned – see Art. 27(2) of Directive 2004/38. The important factor to remember is that the behaviour or activity of that person must be current, and not merely something in that person's past. The following are some key case examples.

**KEY CASE**

**Case 41/74 *Van Duyn* v. *Home Office* [1974] ECR 1337**

*Concerning: exclusion of a migrant worker on grounds of public policy based upon association with a particular group*

**Facts**

Van Duyn was a Dutch woman who wanted to enter the UK to take up a job working within the Church of Scientology in the UK. Although not a banned organisation, it was viewed by the UK government as undesirable. The Home Office refused her entry on grounds that her conduct, as a member of this organisation, was contrary to public policy.

**Legal principle**

The ECJ decided that the concept of public policy had to be interpreted narrowly, but that a Member State had a certain amount of discretion as to how it was to be applied. Therefore van Duyn's *current* membership of this organisation could constitute grounds for refusing her entry, even where it was not a banned organisation. The activity has to be considered 'socially harmful'.

**KEY CASE**

## Case 30/77 *R* v. *Bouchereau* [1977] ECR 1999

*Concerning: criminal convictions as 'conduct' under public policy grounds for exclusion*

### Facts

Mr Bouchereau was a Frenchman who had been convicted on several occasions of drug possession. Because of his convictions, the UK were attempting to expel him, and claimed they were justified in doing so because of his conduct.

### Legal principle

The activities of the person concerned must be socially harmful in order to justify expelling him.

**EXAM TIP**

The important point of the above case is that it's not just a history of criminal convictions that allows a person to be expelled – the longer the time since the conviction, the less likely it is to be relevant. Therefore, it is important to weigh up the seriousness of the criminal offence and how long ago it was committed if faced with a scenario that includes a person with a criminal record.

**KEY CASE**

## Case 67/74 *Bonsignore* v. *Oberstadtdirektor of the City of Cologne* [1975] ECR 297

*Concerning: expulsion under public security used preventatively*

### Facts

Bonsignore was an Italian working in Germany. He was convicted of a minor firearms offence and the German government attempted to deport him back to Italy. They claimed it was in order to deter other immigrants from committing similar offences.

### Legal principle

The argument was rejected. The ECJ said that the reason had to be about the possible future behaviour of that person, not in order generally to prevent others from following his example.

## Public health

This has a broader scope than the other two derogations. According to Art. 29 of Directive 2004/38, it is limited to the following:

- 'Diseases with epidemic potential'
- 'Other infectious diseases or contagious parasitic diseases'

The important thing here is that this is also limited in time (unlike the other two derogations). If a disease is contracted more than 3 months after the worker has entered the country, then it cannot be a reason for expelling them. Also, HIV/AIDS is excepted.

# ■Chapter summary: putting it all together

## Test yourself

☐ Can you tick all the points from the **revision checklist** at the beginning of this chapter?

☐ Attempt the **sample question** from the beginning of this chapter using the answer guidelines below.

☐ Go to the **companion website** to access more revision support online, including interactive quizzes, sample questions with answer guidelines, 'you be the marker' exercises, flashcards and podcasts you can download.

## Answer guidelines

See the problem question at the start of the chapter.

### Approaching the question

This question requires you to consider the rights of three individuals, two of whom are EU nationals while the other is not. You must first consider the rights of the two EU nationals, and then any rights that the non-EU national may have in relation to them. It is important therefore to approach this question in a methodical way, dealing with one person at a time.

## Important points to include

Consider:

- Stefan and Juanita are entitled to live in the UK for up to 3 months looking for work (Art. 6 Directive 2004/38).

- Stefan has found a job, but it is part time, does this allow him to be classed as a worker? See *Levin*.

- Juanita has not found work; can she still be classed as a 'worker'? Consider whether she is entitled to any support in relation to her education under Directive 2004/38 either as a worker, or as part of Stefan's 'family'. Also, consider whether she is entitled to remain in the country either as a 'worker' or as part of Stefan's 'family'. Can she say she is actively seeking work?

- Tatiana is not an EU national, and therefore does not have any rights of free movement as a worker, but is she part of the family of a worker? See Art. 2(2) of Directive 2004/38.

- Can Stefan be deported merely for his association with a suspected drug trafficker? Look at public policy grounds for derogation from free movement of workers under Art. 45(2).

### ✓ Make your answer stand out

You must consider the way in which the ECJ has approached the application of these rules, and not just the rules themselves. A good answer to this question will consider the broad or narrow interpretation placed upon the rights and exceptions in this area in order to provide an accurate application of the law to the facts, which should result in clear advice to the parties concerned. Don't just reiterate facts – remember this is about advising the parties concerned, so you will need to show you understand the rules *and* how they apply.

## READ TO IMPRESS

Castro Oliveira, A. (2002) Workers and Other Persons: Step-by-step from Movement to Citizenship, 39 CML Rev 77

Dougan, M. (2005) Fees, Grants, Loans and Dole Cheques: Who Covers the Cost of Migrant Education within the EU?, 42 CML Rev 943

Woods, L. (1999) Family Rights in the EU – Disadvantaging the Disadvantaged?, 11 *Child & Family Law Quarterly* 17

# NOTES

# Competition law

## Revision checklist

### Essential points you should know:

- [ ] The purpose behind the use of Articles 101 and 102 to regulate competition law in Europe
- [ ] The definitions applied in the Treaty to both Articles 101 and 102
- [ ] The way in which Article 101 is applied to anti-competitive agreements
- [ ] The application of exemptions to Article 101, such as block exemptions and comfort letters
- [ ] The application of Article 102 to anti-competitive abuses of a dominant position

# ■Topic map

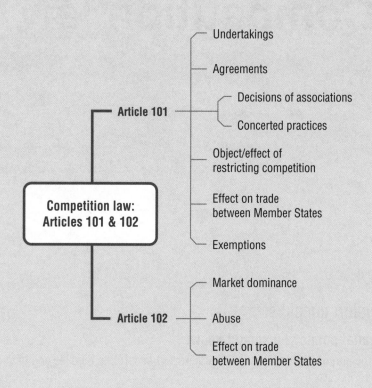

Competition law: Articles 101 & 102

Article 101
- Undertakings
- Agreements
  - Decisions of associations
  - Concerted practices
- Object/effect of restricting competition
- Effect on trade between Member States
- Exemptions

Article 102
- Market dominance
- Abuse
- Effect on trade between Member States

A printable version of this topic map is available from **www.pearsoned.co.uk/lawexpress**

# ■Introduction

**Competition law in Arts. 101 and 102 is just one aspect of the rules set up by the EU to regulate the Single Market.**

The aim is to ensure that there is as free a market as possible, but with enough regulation to ensure that the market is not abused. Articles 101 and 102 are therefore only a part of this, but a key part. These two Treaty Articles prohibit:

■ Anti-competitive agreements between **undertakings** and restrictive practices

■ Abuse by a company of a dominant position in the market

When looking at these rules, it is important to note the context within which they sit: they are part of the measures aimed at the smooth running of the Single European Market, and you should also bear in mind that there are rules for Member States to follow (regarding free movement and the customs union) and also anti-dumping measures, and so although an examination question may not cover all these areas, you should always remember that Arts. 101 and 102 exist in this wider context.

This chapter examines the rules in Arts. 101 and 102, and looks at how they have been applied in practice through the case law. This should therefore allow you to consider the use of these rules in a practical context (useful for problem questions) and also their more theoretical aspects (useful for essay questions).

## ASSESSMENT ADVICE

Questions on this area of law can vary according to the way in which competition law is taught at your university, as the focus of the subject can vary greatly.

**Problem questions** are probably the most straightforward to deal with, as they will be looking for the application of the law to the scenario outlined in the question. As EU competition law is heavily based on the criteria in Arts. 101 and 102, this can be a fairly straightforward exercise if you are also prepared to discuss a range of cases that help to illustrate the application of these principles.

**Essay questions** will also call for knowledge of the cases, as the question will require knowledge of this area beyond the rules and definitions in the Treaty.

# ■ Sample question

Could you answer this question? Below is a typical essay question that could arise on this topic. Guidelines on answering the question are included at the end of this chapter, whilst a sample problem question and guidance on tackling it can be found on the companion website.

## ESSAY QUESTION

Critically evaluate the effect of the introduction of Regulation 1/2003 on Art. 101. Does the new system under this Regulation have any advantages beyond merely reducing the workload of the Commission in granting individual exemptions?

# ■ Article 101: anti-competitive agreements between undertakings

### KEY STATUTE

**Articles 101(1) and (2) TFEU**

(1) The following shall be prohibited as incompatible with the common market: all agreements between undertakings, decisions by associations of undertakings and concerted practices which may affect trade between Member States and which have as their object or effect the prevention, restriction or distortion of competition within the common market, and in particular those which:

    (a) directly or indirectly fix purchase or selling prices or any other trading conditions;

    (b) limit or control production, markets, technical development, or investment;

    (c) share markets or sources of supply;

    (d) apply dissimilar conditions to equivalent transactions with other trading parties, thereby placing them at a competitive disadvantage;

    (e) make the conclusion of contracts subject to acceptance by the other parties of supplementary obligations which, by their nature or according to commercial usage, have no connection with the subject of such contracts.

(2) Any agreements or decisions prohibited pursuant to this Article shall be automatically void.

Article 101's purpose is to prevent any restrictive practices which may have an effect on competition in the EU (Figure 8.1). It is very specific about the type of activities it includes (those listed under (a) to (e) in the extract from Art. 101 above), although this list is not exhaustive. In order to understand Art. 101, you need to break it down into its different parts.

## To whom does Article 101 apply?

Article 101 is aimed at private bodies, or **'undertakings'** as it says in the Treaty. It is *not* there to deal with the activities of governments or the public sector – they are dealt with by other parts of the Treaty.

**Figure 8.1**

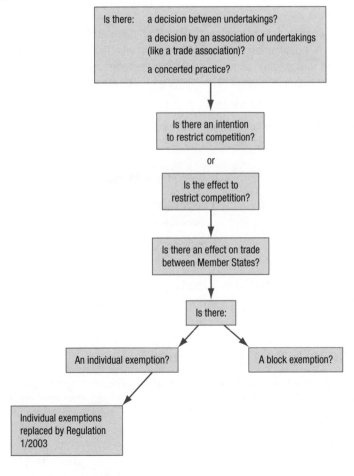

**KEY DEFINITION: Undertakings**

This is intended to cover only private individuals, and so it means natural persons (such as you and I) or legal persons (companies). However, in the context of Art. 101, it has also been defined as groups of companies too.

**KEY CASE**

Case C-159/91 *Pucet* v. *Assurances Générales de France* [1993] ECR I-637

*Concerning: definition of 'undertaking'*

**Facts**

This case concerned accusations that a regional social security organisation had been anti-competitive regarding social insurance 'services'.

**Legal principle**

In deciding whether a body was an 'undertaking', the Court of Justice decided that there was a distinction to be made based on whether the body concerned was engaged in economic activities as such, or whether, as in this case, the body pursued activities on the basis of solidarity and with no intention to make a profit.

Some examples of bodies considered by the ECJ as to whether they are 'undertakings' under Art. 101 are shown in the following table.

| Case | Is it an 'undertaking'? |
| --- | --- |
| Case C-343/95 *Diego Cali* v. *SEPG* | A body established by national law (in this case to collect harbour duties) was not an undertaking |
| Case C-364/92 *SAT* v. *Eurocontrol* | A body set up by Treaty was not an undertaking |
| Case C-519/04P *Meca-Medina and Majcen* v. *Commission* | A sporting body (such as the International Olympic Committee) could be an undertaking |

# What does Article 101 prohibit?

There are three broad categories of what the Article prohibits: 'agreements between undertakings, decisions by associations of undertakings and concerted practices'.

| Activity | Meaning |
|---|---|
| Agreements between undertakings | Can be both binding/non-binding, written or verbal. Can even include 'gentlemen's agreements' |
| Decisions by associations of undertakings | Binding or non-binding instructions/recommendations by trade associations to members |
| Concerted practices | Action by competitors in a market arising from them coordinating their actions, such as coordinated price rises by different companies where there is no other plausible explanation other than the concerted practice |

This means that Art. 101 can have a broad coverage. Some examples of what can fall within the different categories follow.

## Agreements

| Case | Agreement |
|---|---|
| Case 32/78 *BMW Belgium* v. *Commission* | Belgian car dealers signed a document agreeing to the manufacturer's request not to sell cars in other Member States |
| Case C–338/00 *Volkswagen* v. *Commission* | A telephone call by the manufacturer to car dealers instructing them not to do something |
| Case IV/35.733 *Community* v. *Volkswagen AG and Others* | Request to car dealers not to re-export cars (even though the car dealers' compliance was extracted by heavy pressure) |

## Decisions by associations of undertakings

This is where a trade association will issue a set of instructions to its members or make an agreement with its members, for example, fixing prices on products sold by its members, as this can allow dominant sellers in the market to keep their dominant position and prevent other companies from competing with them.

## Concerted practices

Although in the first two examples there has to be evidence of an agreement in place, the idea of concerted practices is a lot wider, although it is still down to the Commission to get evidence to show that what is happening is a concerted practice, and not just everyone raising their prices when one company does, as happens with petrol prices. There has to be consistent evidence of a concerted practice, but that can be one of a number of things, to conclusively be considered a concerted practice. See the following key case.

**KEY CASE**

**Case 11, 40–8, 50, 56, 113-4/73** *Suiker Unie* v. *Commission* **[1975] ECR 1663**
*Concerning: meaning of 'concerted practice'*

**Facts**

Sugar producers in the EU had decided only to import into Holland with permission from the main Dutch producers. Doing this meant that there was less pressure on the Dutch sugar producers to compete than there would have been had the other producers just imported into the country without their permission. They were accused of engaging in a concerted practice, but claimed they were not because there was no agreement between the different sugar producers to do this.

**Legal principle**

The ECJ held that it was not necessary for there to be a specific understanding in order for this to be a concerted practice. It just needed to involve some sort of contact, whether it be direct or indirect, which led to the action (like price-fixing) taking place. A concerted practice allows competitors to fix a position in the knowledge of what others are going to do.

# Object or effect of restricting competition

In some situations it is possible to show that there was intention to restrict competition, but even if this is not the case, if it can be shown that the effect (whether intended or not) was to restrict competition, then this will be enough.

**EXAM TIP**

Remember when looking at this issue that if you are dealing with a problem question, you need to look at the effect *within the relevant market*, so it is important to be able to define the relevant product market, or the relevant geographical area. A relevant market may be broad, for example 'fruit', or it may be narrow, for example 'bananas'.

There are also two types of agreement that can have an effect on the relevant market, and Art. 101 applies to both of them:

| Type of agreement | Definition |
|---|---|
| Vertical agreements | Between those on different levels, e.g. imposed upon a distributor by the supplier |
| Horizontal agreements | Between firms that operate on the same level in the market |

**KEY CASE**

**Case 56 & 58/64 *Consten* v. *Commission* [1966] ECR 299**

*Concerning: types of agreements covered by Article 101*

**Facts**

This case concerned an agreement between a supplier and their distributor for products to be sold in France. An agreement was made between them that the distributor would not sell outside France, and in return the supplier agreed to make agreements with its other European distributors that they would not sell in France. The agreement was challenged under Art. 101 when another distributor (from Germany) started selling the products in France at a lower price.

**Legal principle**

The ECJ decided that the agreement was contrary to Art. 101, and in doing so, it made several important points:

■ Article 101 could apply to vertical agreements (as this one was) as well as horizontal ones
■ The fact that this agreement had streamlined and increased distribution of the product in question was irrelevant
■ The important point here was that the agreement had harmed the Single European Market by an attempt to repartition along national boundaries.

# Examples of what is prohibited in Article 101(1)

The list in Art. 101(1) is not meant to be exclusive – there are other things which potentially could breach Art. 101 *if* they meet the criteria discussed above. However, they are a good starting point. They are as follows:

(a) directly or indirectly fix purchase or selling prices or any other trading conditions;
(b) limit or control production, markets, technical development, or investment;
(c) share markets or sources of supply;

(d) apply dissimilar conditions to equivalent transactions with other trading parties, thereby placing them at a competitive disadvantage;

(e) make the conclusion of contracts subject to acceptance by the other parties of supplementary obligations which, by their nature or according to commercial usage, have no connection with the subject of such contracts.

# Effect on trade between Member States

**! Don't be tempted to...**

You must be wary of assuming that action can be taken in trivial circumstances (referred to as situations of *de minimis.*) Both Arts. 101 and 102 deal with activities that may affect free competition within the EU. However, not all agreements or abuses may be subject to this rule. Have a look at Case 5/69 *Volk* v. *Vervaecke* [1969] ECR 295, where it was decided that the agreement didn't breach Art. 101 because it didn't have a significant effect on the market. (The effect was *de minimis.*) However, in Case 23/67 *Brasserie de Haecht* v. *Wilkin* [1967] ECR 407, if there are several agreements which when added together do have a significant effect, then they will breach Art. 101.

In order for something to satisfy this aspect of Art. 101, it must either have:

■ A direct or indirect effect on trade between Member States or

■ The capability of such an effect

This is a very wide definition, and is made wider still by the fact that the term 'trade' is also given a very wide meaning (although as can be seen regarding the definition of 'undertaking' mentioned earlier in this chapter, economic activity is important), but significantly, if it doesn't affect trade between Member States, then it should be dealt with by national law, and not EU law.

# Exemptions from Article 101

It is possible for an agreement under Art. 101 not to be declared void if it fulfils *all* of the following conditions:

■ It contributes to improving production or distribution of goods or to promoting technical or economic progress

■ It allows consumers a fair share of this benefit

■ It does not impose conditions that are not necessary to achieve the above

■ It does not allow undertakings to eliminate a substantial amount of competition

# Application of exemptions

There were previously three ways of gaining an exemption:

| Method of exemption | Explanation |
| --- | --- |
| Individual exemption | Application to the Commission for a decision as to whether the agreement falls within Art. 101(3). This has now been removed by Reg. 1/2003 |
| Comfort letter | An alternative to the individual decision, this is an informal opinion from the Commission that the agreement does not breach Art. 101. Saves time, but is non-binding and has no legal effect. Also now essentially defunct |
| Block exemption | Blanket exemptions in certain industries passed by regulation. Again, this saves Commission time, by allowing blanket exemption in industries where it is recognised that the majority of agreements should be exempted, for example certain types of vertical agreements |

 Make your answer stand out

Regulation 1/2003 changed the existing system of individual notification and comfort letters. These procedures took a lot of the Commission's time, and so the Regulation devolved the matter down to national level. This was done by making Art. 101(3) directly effective, and so it allowed companies themselves to resolve any problems in *national* courts of Member States. Cases decided under the old system are still relevant, and can still be used in answering assessment questions in this area. The new system was brought into force on 1 May 2004, in time for the accession of 10 new states – if it had not taken effect, then the Commission would probably have been completely overloaded with work from the new Member States.

The only drawback is that the Regulation has removed the comfort previously given by the Commission taking responsibility for this area. However, it has allowed national courts to deal with these matters.

If you are dealing with an issue in a problem question, please make sure that you do not advise the party concerned to get an individual exemption as this is now no longer relevant. If you are addressing an essay question which asks you to critically discuss the subject, then you can make your answer stand out by showing that you appreciate the change in this area. Knowing a little bit about ▶

the previous system may allow you to show an appreciation of the change that has taken place.

See Roitman (2006); Saunders (2006); and Venit (2003).

---

**EXAM TIP**

Although Art. 101 presents itself as a list of criteria to fulfil, it is still important to make sure you are able to discuss examples from the cases. Examiners will be looking for depth of knowledge, and the amount you understand of how Art. 101 operates will come through in your answer.

---

# ■ Article 102: abuse of a dominant position

**KEY STATUTE**

**Article 102(1) TFEU**

Any abuse by one or more undertakings of a dominant position within the common market or in a substantial part of it shall be prohibited as incompatible with the common market in so far as it may affect trade between Member States.

---

Unlike Art. 101, Art. 102 tends to involve just one company abusing a strong position in the marketplace in which they are working. (It can involve several companies working together to produce a combined dominance.) Therefore, in order to deal with this area, you need to define several important elements. Art. 102 just requires:

- An undertaking (see the definition under Art. 101)
- A dominant position
- Abuse of that dominant position
- Effect on trade between Member States

If all of these elements are present, then there is a breach of Art. 102.

# Market dominance

**KEY CASE**

**Case 27/76 *United Brands* v. *Commission* [1978] ECR 207**

*Concerning: definition of a dominant position*

**Facts**

United Brands were importers of bananas. They imposed various terms on the companies they supplied, for example insisting that bananas were not sold while still green, charging different prices to different suppliers in different countries, and in some circumstances, refusing to supply bananas. They were accused by the Commission of abusing a dominant position in their market.

**Legal principle**

A dominant position was defined as being a position of economic strength which allowed two things: (i) the dominant undertaking to *hinder effective competition*, and (ii) the undertaking to *act independently* of its competitors and consumers.

In order to establish this dominance, it is important to look at the relevant market. For example, in *United Brands*, the court had to decide whether the relevant market was for bananas or more generally for fruit. To establish what the market is, you need to look at the following:

| Market | Explanation |
|---|---|
| Relevant product market (RPM) | Two important factors: the ability to substitute your product for other similar products, and the similarity of your products to other products |
| Geographical market | You need to consider how large a geographical area the company operates in. It must be 'the common market or a substantial part of it' |

These issues then feed into a consideration of how dominant the undertaking is. For example:

Case 27/76 *United Brands* v. *Commission*: United Brands were dominant because the RPM was 'bananas', and not more generally 'fruit'. Bananas were different enough from other fruit for them not to be cross-substitutable. In considering this issue, you need to bear in mind something called 'demand-side substitutability'. Other fruit could not substitute bananas, and this led to a very narrow market definition.

Case T-83/91 *Tetra-Pak* v. *Commission* [1994] ECR II-755: the relevant geographical market was the whole of the EU.

*B&I Line* v. *Sealink Harbours & Stena Sealink* [1992] 5 CMLR 255: because the market concerned the control of harbours (rather limited because of the number of harbours in the EU) then a single harbour was a substantial part of the geographical market.

Cases C-241/91 and C-242/91P *RTE and ITP* v. *Commission*: the market here was defined as the market for TV listings information on BBC and RTE programmes, and therefore was narrow as in *United Brands*.

Case T-229/94 *Deutsche Bahn AG* v. *Commission*: in this case, the relevant market was for the carriage of marine containers by rail and therefore was very specific.

## Dominance as a fact

These factors then feed into the issue of dominance as a fact. This can be as simple as merely having more of a share in the market than anyone else. It can be a case of having a larger share of the market than everyone else combined. Here are some examples:

| Case | Situation of dominance |
|------|------------------------|
| Case 85/76 *Hoffman la Roche* v. *Commission* [1979] ECR 1869 | 70–80% share in the market |
| Case 27/76 *United Brands* v. *Commission* [1978] ECR 207 | 40–45% share in the market |
| Case T–219/99 *British Airways* v. *Commission* [2004] All ER (EC) 1115 | 39.7% share in the market, where the nearest competitor, Virgin, had 5.5% share |

**EXAM TIP**

Dominance can be relative, as shown by the *British Airways* case in the table above. BA had less than half the share in its market that Hoffman la Roche did in their case, but because BA's nearest rival had a much smaller share, they were still dominant. Think when you consider if an undertaking is dominant, rather than just seeing if they have the majority (over 50%) of the market.

**!** **Don't be tempted to...**

Don't think that the market share in itself is the only consideration when looking at market dominance. There are other considerations that the Court will also take into account when considering this issue. This includes the possibility of the undertaking having large financial resources (either their own, or access to other monies) or the possibility of having a technological advantage over competitors and therefore the ability to stay ahead in product development.

# Abuse

Dominance on its own is *not* a breach of Art. 102. However, the abuse of that dominant position is. There is a non-exclusive list of examples in Art. 102.

**KEY STATUTE**

**Article 102(2) TFEU**

Such abuse may, in particular, consist in:

(a) directly or indirectly imposing unfair purchase or selling prices or other unfair trading conditions;
(b) limiting production, markets or technical development to the prejudice of consumers;
(c) applying dissimilar conditions to equivalent transactions with other trading parties, thereby placing them at a competitive disadvantage;
(d) making the conclusion of contracts subject to acceptance by the other parties of supplementary obligations which, by their nature or according to commercial usage, have no connection with the subject of such contracts.

The *United Brands* case is such a good case to apply here, because they were actually doing all four of the things listed above! There are other examples, though, and some of these are listed in the table overleaf.

The key thing to remember here is that all of these are examples of where someone has a dominant position, and is doing something which is abusive that exploits that dominant position. This is the key to breach of Art. 102. Also bear in mind that the ECJ has said that activities which allow an undertaking to achieve dominance that would be damaging to competition are also covered by Art. 102 – see Case 6/72 *Europemballage and Continental Can* v. *Commission*.

| Case | Abuse |
| --- | --- |
| Case 226/84 *British Leyland* v. *Commission* [1986] ECR 3263 | Unfair prices: charging more for approval certificates for left-hand drive cars |
| Case 238/87 *Volvo* v. *Eric Veng* [1988] ECR 6211 | Limiting the market: use of intellectual property rights to prevent competitors from producing spare parts for Volvo cars |
| Case T-219/99 *British Airways* v. *Commission* [2004] All ER (EC) 1115 | Discrimination: use of a dominant position in the market for travel agents to discriminate between levels of commission paid to agents |
| Case 85/76 *Hoffman la Roche* v. *Commission* [1979] ECR 1869 | Tying in: a tying-in clause stopped suppliers from buying from Hoffman's competitors, and allowed them to control the market |
| Case T-70/89 *Radio Telefis Eireann* v. *Commission* [1991] ECR II-485 | Refusal to supply: RTE and BBC refused to license TV listings information to competitors, therefore preventing competition for TV listings magazines |

 Make your answer stand out

The *RTE* case above seems to have led to an 'essential facilities doctrine', where if an undertaking refuses to license or supply (on reasonable terms) something which is considered an 'essential facility' then this can also be an abuse. This has a particular effect on those companies that produce things which cannot be reproduced by their competitors. This appears to put a higher level of control on companies that are in this position. Bear this in mind if dealing with a problem question that appears to involve a company that makes something that their competitors cannot make themselves.

See Stothers (2001).

# Effect on trade between Member States

The effect of a breach on trade between Member States seems to have been very widely construed, as with Art. 101, to prevent it obstructing the use of Art. 102. Any effect on the market between Member States is enough.

**EXAM TIP**

The issues of the market and whether a company is dominant or not are ones to be dealt with on an individual basis, so it is important for you to be able to *apply* the law rather than just present the criteria in your answer.

# ■Chapter summary: putting it all together

## Test yourself

- ☐ Can you tick all the points from the **revision checklist** at the beginning of this chapter?
- ☐ Attempt the **sample question** from the beginning of this chapter using the answer guidelines below.
- ☐ Go to the **companion website** to access more revision support online, including interactive quizzes, sample questions with answer guidelines, 'you be the marker' exercises, flashcards and podcasts you can download.

## Answer guidelines

See the essay question at the start of the chapter.

### Approaching the question

The question itself appears to be very specific in its focus, but don't let this mislead you. A wider appreciation of Art. 101 and how it operates will also need to be discussed in order to allow you to evaluate how Reg. 1/2003 has affected the way in which it works.

### Important points to include

You will need to discuss:

- ■ The requirements of Art. 101, in particular the criteria for breach of this Article
- ■ The type of agreements considered to breach Art. 101
- ■ The exceptions listed under Art. 101(3)

■ Examples of how these have been applied under the previous system of comfort letters and individual notification

■ The consequences of removing control over Art. 101 from the Commission – see Reg. 1/2003

✓ **Make your answer stand out**

The temptation here will be merely to follow the flow diagram provided in this chapter and take a 'write everything you know about' approach to answering this question. However, this will not address the core of what it is asking you, and therefore you need to think about how the working knowledge you have of Art. 81 allows you to produce an informed answer. Also – *very* importantly – your appreciation of how the law has developed here will also help. A sophisticated appreciation of how the law has changed, and why, will help you to show you have a critical understanding of this area.

## READ TO IMPRESS

Korah, V. (1980) Concept of a Dominant Position Within the Meaning of Article 86, 17 CML Rev 395

Roitman, D. (2006) Legal Uncertainty for Vertical Distribution Agreements: The Block Exemption Regulation 2790/1999 (BER) and Related Aspects of the New Regulation 1/2003, 27 ECLR 261

Saunders, O.O.R. (2006) Regulation 1/2003 – An Effective Mechanism for Managing Economic and Monetary Union in an Enlarged Community?, 27 Bus LR 148

Stothers, C. (2001) Refusal to Supply as Abuse of a Dominant Position: The Essential Facilities Doctrine in the European Union, 22(7) ECLR 256

Venit, J.S. (2003) Brave New World: The Modernisation and Decentralisation of Enforcement under Articles 81 and 82 of the EC Treaty, 40 CMLR 545

Vogelaar, F. (2005) European Competition Law Revisited: the 'Great Overhaul' of 2004 Analysed, 32 Legal IEI 105

**NOTES**

**NOTES**

# And finally, before the exam ...

By using this book to direct your revision, you should now have a good grasp of the way in which the EU operates, and the key areas of substantive law. Remember that the information contained in this guide is not intended to substitute for your own notes and textbook reading, but to help to point you in the right direction when using these sources, which are going to have much more depth and detail than can be included here. Most importantly, you should check to make sure you have *understood* the different topic areas covered, as this will be crucial to success. EU law requires you to understand how the system operates as well as how the law is applied.

## Test yourself

- [ ] Look at the **revision checklists** at the start of each chapter. Are you happy that you can now tick them all? If not, go back to the particular chapter and work through the material again. If you are still struggling, seek help from your tutor.
- [ ] Go to the **companion website** and revisit the online resources.
  - [ ] Take the full **study plan** test to assess your knowledge in all areas.
  - [ ] Try the **practice quizzes** and see if you can score full marks for each chapter.
  - [ ] Attempt to answer the **sample questions** for each chapter within the time limit.
  - [ ] Use the **flashcards** to test your recall of the legal principles of the cases and statutes you've revised and the definitions of important terms.

☐ See if you can spot the strengths and weaknesses of the sample answers in '**you be the marker**'.

☐ Listen to the **podcast** and then attempt the question it discusses.

☐ If you are having problems with case names, remember that they are often abbreviated in a common way by all textbook writers and lecturers: e.g. *R* v. *Secretary of State for Transport ex parte Factortame* is commonly just referred to as '*Factortame*'.

☐ If you are allowed to take a statute book in to the exam, make sure you are familiar with the EC Treaty, and its numbering. All Articles relating to a particular subject tend to be grouped together: e.g. all powers of the European Commission are contained in Arts. 244–250 TFEU, and all Articles relating to the free movement of goods and customs union are in Arts. 34–37.

# ■ Linking it all up

Check where there are overlaps between subject areas. (You may want to review the 'revision note' boxes throughout this book.) Make a careful note of these as knowing how one topic may lead into another can increase your marks significantly. Here are some examples:

✓ Overlap between one of the free movement areas and Art. 258, because this question will be about both the law itself and the action that can be taken to enforce that law.

✓ Sources of law areas can overlap with Art. 267 (interpretation by the ECJ), because this will concern the way in which an individual may be able to enforce law in national courts.

✓ Questions concerning the powers of the Institutions can overlap with specific procedures that may be used by those Institutions – e.g. Art. 263 (judicial review) is a specific example of how any of the primary Institutions can exercise their powers to supervise the other Institutions' activities.

# ■ Sample question

Below is an essay question that incorporates overlapping areas of the law. See if you can answer this question drawing upon your knowledge of the whole subject area. Guidelines on answering this question are included at the end of this section.

## ESSAY QUESTION

On 1 March 1999 the European Commission resigned to avoid the European Parliament exercising its power of censure against it. This power is a key aspect of the checks and balances system that has been developing at EU level with the changes made by Treaties over the past 30 years.

Discuss this system and evaluate how satisfactory it is at monitoring the activity within the EU.

# Answer guidelines

## Approaching the question

This question is designed to pull in several subjects and test your ability to draw links between the different areas of EU law in a discussion of the system. It is focused upon the supervisory powers of the Institutions, but in order to fully answer the question, you also need to make sure that other overlapping areas are also covered.

## Important points to include

The following are issues you will need to consider in dealing with this question:

- The system the question mentions has developed with changes made by the Single European Act, the Maastricht Treaty, the Treaty of Amsterdam, the Treaty of Nice and the Treaty of Lisbon.

- Specific examples from the above Treaties focus on the powers of the Parliament, so discuss their powers of supervision and censure over the Commission, and possible reasons behind it, and their powers to monitor the Council of Ministers through questioning.

- The Council of Ministers also has its own powers, for example, their power of appointment of the Commission.

- The increased involvement of the Parliament in making law has allowed it to have a greater say in the law-making process, so you can discuss the procedures of cooperation and codecision here. The recent Lisbon changes in particular can be discussed.

- Articles 263 and 265 (judicial review) allow any of the Institutions to challenge improper procedural actions under the Treaty and also form part of the system of checks and balances. The grounds for challenge are relevant here, and therefore it will allow you to evaluate how effective this is as part of the system of checks and balances.

■ Your evaluation of the EU system will dictate the answer you produce – but it is worth bearing in mind that although this is a question which covers several areas, you should remain focused upon the question. This is *not* about writing everything you know about this area – it requires a critical discussion.

 Make your answer stand out

This is an ever-changing area, particularly at the moment, due to the speed of EU reform. Therefore your answer won't necessarily be the same as that provided by students in previous years. You must make sure that you take account of the Lisbon reforms, and make sure that your information in revising for exam questions is up-to-date. By making your knowledge as current as possible, you will be able to show you have taken on board all the recent changes. An appreciation of the effect of politics upon the EU will help you produce a high quality answer.

## NOTES

# Glossary of terms

The glossary is divided into two parts: key definitions and other useful terms. The key definitions can be found within the chapter in which they occur as well as here below. These definitions are the essential terms that you must know and understand in order to prepare for an exam. The additional list of terms provides further definitions of useful terms and phrases which will also help you answer examination and coursework questions effectively. These terms are highlighted in the text as they occur but the definition can only be found here.

## ■ Key definitions

| | |
|---|---|
| *Acte clair* | A condition under which an issue of EU law is clear and does not need to be clarified by the ECJ |
| **Court of last instance** | In a court structure, this is the very last or highest court that a particular case can reach |
| **Court or tribunal** | Generally a court or tribunal is one that has a judicial function, and independence from the parties concerned |
| **Democratic deficit** | The accusation that the EU lacks democracy, due to a lack of democratic accountability to individual citizens. This has been partially addressed by the direct elections in the European Parliament |
| **Derogation** | The exemption from, or the relaxation of, a particular law |
| **Dualist** | A dualist legal system is one where international agreements also have to be passed by the national parliament |
| **Goods** | Goods are interpreted as 'products which can be valued in money and which are capable, as such, of forming the subject of commercial transactions'. (Case 7/68 *Re Export Tax on Art.* |

|  | *Treasures: EC Commission* v *Italy* (1968) ECR 423 at 428) |
|---|---|
| **Horizontal effect** | A piece of EU legislation has horizontal effect where it is enforceable by an individual against another individual |
| **Indistinctly applicable measures** | These are restrictions or other measures which apply equally to imported products and domestic products |
| **Legislative power** | The power of the Institutions to make law |
| **Making a reference** | Under Art. 267, where a national court sends questions to the ECJ for interpretation |
| **Negative duty** | A duty not to do something |
| **Qualified majority voting** | Qualified majority voting is a form of voting where a certain percentage of the total vote must be in favour, usually around two-thirds |
| **Reasoned opinion** | Under Art. 258, the reasoned opinion is a written statement from the Commission which lays down the obligation concerned, and the reasons why the Member State has failed to meet this obligation. It should clearly spell out the Commission's objection, and therefore it should be possible for the Member State to know what it needs to do to rectify this situation |
| **Supervisory power** | The power of the Institutions to supervise each other |
| **Undertakings** | This is intended to cover only private individuals, and so it means natural persons (such as you and I) or legal persons (companies). However, in the context of Art. 101, it has also been defined as groups of companies too |
| **Vertical effect** | A piece of EU legislation has vertical effect where it is enforceable by an individual against the State |
| **Worker** | Workers are EU nationals who are either in employment (full or part time) in that they are paid in return for their performance under an employer/employee relationship, or are seeking actual paid work |

# ■ Other useful terms

| | |
|---|---|
| *Acquis communitaire* | The existing body of EU law, all cases and legislation, both primary and secondary |
| **Adversarial** | A procedure where the parties concerned present their own evidence and the court decides the case based upon this |
| **Community Act** | Any legislation made under EU law, whether Treaties or secondary legislation under Art. 288 |
| *Locus standi* | A condition under which an individual or other entity has the permission or status to bring a case before the ECJ |
| **MEQR** | Measures equivalent to quantitative restrictions |
| **Primary legislation** | In the EU context, this is Treaty law agreed by the Member States |
| **Secondary legislation** | Law made by the institutions under the powers given to them in Art. 288 |
| **Unity principle** | This is the principle where both Arts. 263 and 265 are dealt with consistently by the ECJ. |

# Index

**Emboldened** entries refer to those appearing in the glossary